EVERYTHING   DID

EVERYTHING JESUS SAID AND DID

As recorded in the Bible

Taken from the
New International Version,
Inclusive Language Edition

Hodder & Stoughton
LONDON SYDNEY AUCKLAND

British Library Cataloguing in Publication Data
A record for this book is available from the British Library

ISBN 0 340 65199 7

Designed and typeset by Watermark, Norfolk
Printed and bound in Great Britain by
Cox & Wyman Ltd, Reading, Berks.

Hodder & Stoughton Ltd
A Division of Hodder Headline PLC
338 Euston Road
London NW1 3BH

Contents

THE TEACHING OF JESUS

WORDS OF THE RISEN LORD

PART 2   WHAT JESUS DID

THE LIFE OF JESUS

THE HEALINGS OF JESUS

PART 3 *WHAT JESUS PRAYED*

Introduction

Monty Python's *Life of Brian* was originally planned to parody the life of Jesus. But the story goes that when the Python team began to look through the Bible for material they could use, much to their surprise, they discovered that their desire to mock Jesus soon evaporated. In fact, they realised that they actually *liked* him. What they *didn't* like was all the clutter which they felt had obscured him from people through the ages. In my work as a church leader and television presenter, I come across literally hundreds of people who feel exactly the same. They may not know that much about Jesus, but they like what they do know . . . and would be very interested in knowing more – if only it were possible without all the smells, bells, sermons and hype!

If you're the same way, then this book is for you. Perhaps you want to know more about Jesus, but just can't seem to make head nor tail of what goes on in church. Perhaps you'd like to know what he said and did, but find the thought of struggling through the Bible more than a little daunting. Perhaps you've heard all sorts of things about Jesus and what he taught and want to find out whether they're true or not.

After all, when you stop to think about it, it's really quite odd that Jesus, the son of a poor Palestinian carpenter who lived 2,000 years ago and was born in a cow shed, should be so famous! What is even stranger is that, though he never wrote a book, had no formal qualifications, was never appointed to political office, never travelled more than 200 miles from his birthplace, and was executed by the Roman government for treason, he has, beyond doubt, influenced history more than any other human being who has ever lived. For instance, his birthday is the basis for our whole dating system: this book has been published 1996 years after his birth.

Schools, hospitals and colleges have been built across the world in his honour – not to mention the churches, abbeys and cathedrals. And the Bible, which tells his story, is still the world's number one bestseller by a very long way.

Whatever your interest, I think you'll find *Everything Jesus Said And Did* helpful. It takes the words and actions of Jesus straight from the Bible, and lays them out in an easy-to-read format which lets him speak for himself. I am certain that, like countless thousands of others, you'll find it an eye-opening experience.

Steve Chalke
Oasis Trust
London

PART 1

WHAT JESUS SAID

✥ SAYINGS OF JESUS ✥

A. Promises

1. 'God so loved the world'

'For God so loved the world that he gave his one and only Son, that whoever believes in him shall not perish but have eternal life.' JOHN 3:16

2. The kingdom

'Do not be afraid, little flock, for your Father has been pleased to give you the kingdom.' LUKE 12:32

3. Rest

'Come to me, all you who are weary and burdened, and I will give you rest. Take my yoke upon you and learn from me, for I am gentle and humble in heart, and you will find rest for your souls. For my yoke is easy and my burden is light.' MATTHEW 11:28–30

4. Faith

'Everything is possible for one who believes.' MARK 9:23

5. From death to life

'I tell you the truth, those who hear my word and believe him who sent me have eternal life and will not be condemned; they have crossed over from death to life.' JOHN 5:24

6. 'You will know the truth'

'If you hold to my teaching, you are really my disciples. Then you will know the truth, and the truth will set you free.'   JOHN 8:31–32

7. 'Come to me and drink'

On the last and greatest day of the Feast, Jesus stood and said in a loud voice, 'Let anyone who is thirsty come to me and drink. Whoever believes in me, as the Scripture has said, will have streams of living water flowing from within.'   JOHN 7:37–38

8. Answered prayer

'If you believe, you will receive whatever you ask for in prayer.'   MATTHEW 21:22

9. Binding and loosing

'I tell you the truth, whatever you bind on earth will be bound in heaven, and whatever you loose on earth will be loosed in heaven.'   MATTHEW 18:18

B. Commands

1. The golden rule

'In everything, do to others what you would have them do to you, for this sums up the Law and the Prophets.'   MATTHEW 7:12

2. Be generous

'Give, and it will be given to you. A good measure, pressed down, shaken together and running over, will be poured into your lap.'   LUKE 6:38

3. Go through the narrow gate

'Enter through the narrow gate. For wide is the gate and broad is the road that leads to destruction, and many enter through it. But small is the gate and narrow the road that leads to life, and only a few find it.'   MATTHEW 7:13–14

4. 'Ask the Lord . . . to send out workers'

Jesus went through all the towns and villages, teaching in their synagogues, preaching the good news of the kingdom and healing every disease and sickness. When he saw the crowds, he had compassion on them, because they were harassed and helpless, like sheep without a shepherd.

Then he said to his disciples, 'The harvest is plentiful but the workers are few. Ask the Lord of the harvest, therefore, to send out workers into his harvest field.'   MATTHEW 9:35–38

5. Forgive

'Forgive, and you will be forgiven.'   LUKE 6:37

C. Warnings

1. 'Watch out for false prophets'

'Watch out for false prophets. They come to you in sheep's clothing, but inwardly they are ferocious wolves. By their fruit you will recognise them. Do people pick grapes from thorn bushes, or figs from thistles? Likewise every good tree bears good fruit, but a bad tree bears bad fruit. A good tree cannot bear bad fruit, and a bad tree cannot bear good fruit. Every tree that does not bear good fruit is cut down and thrown into the fire. Thus, by their fruit you will recognise them.'   MATTHEW 7:15–20

2. The cost of following Jesus

'The Son of Man has nowhere to lay his head'
As they were walking along the road, someone said to him [Jesus], 'I will follow you wherever you go.'

Jesus replied, 'Foxes have holes and birds of the air have nests, but the Son of Man has nowhere to lay his head.'

'Let me bury my father'
He said to another man, 'Follow me.'

But he replied, 'Lord, first let me go and bury my father.'

Jesus said to him, 'Let the dead bury their own dead, but you go and proclaim the kingdom of God.'

'First let me go back and say good-bye to my family'
Still another said, 'I will follow you, Lord; but first let me go back and say good-bye to my family.'

Jesus replied, 'No-one who takes hold of the plough and looks back is fit for service in the kingdom of God.'   LUKE 9:57–62

3. Being ashamed of Jesus

'All who are ashamed of me and my words, the Son of Man will be ashamed of them when he comes in his glory and in the glory of the Father and of the holy angels.'   LUKE 9:26

4. The condition of following Jesus

'Follow me'
'Those who would come after me must deny themselves and take up their cross and follow me. For those who want to save their lives will lose them, but those who lose their lives for me will find them.'

What can you give in exchange for your soul?
'What good will it be for you to gain the whole world, yet forfeit your soul? Or what can you give in exchange for your soul?'

Rewards according to actions
'For the Son of Man is going to come in his Father's glory with his angels, and then he will reward everyone according to what they have done. I tell you the truth, some who are standing here will not taste death before they see the Son of Man coming in his kingdom.'   MATTHEW 16:24–28

D. Other sayings

1. 'It is more blessed to give than to receive'

[Paul said,] 'In everything I did, I showed you that by this kind of hard work we must help the weak, remembering the words the Lord Jesus himself said: "It is more blessed to give than to receive."'   ACTS 20:35

2. The unforgivable sin

'Whoever is not with me is against me, and whoever does not gather with me scatters. And so I tell you, people will be forgiven every sin and blasphemy. But the blasphemy against the Spirit will not be forgiven. Anyone who speaks a word against the Son of Man will be forgiven, but anyone who speaks against the Holy Spirit will not be forgiven, either in this age or in the age to come.'   MATTHEW 12:30–32

3. Rejection of Jesus' disciples

'Whoever listens to you listens to me; whoever rejects you rejects me; but whoever rejects me rejects him who sent me.'   LUKE 10:16

4. Knowing the Son, knowing the Father

'All things have been committed to me by my Father. No-one knows the Son except the Father, and no-one knows the Father except the Son and those to whom the Son chooses to reveal him.'   MATTHEW 11:27

5. The return of the evil spirit

'When an evil spirit comes out of anyone, it goes through arid places seeking rest and does not find it. Then it says, "I will return to the house I left." When it arrives, it finds the house unoccupied, swept clean and put in order. Then it goes and takes with it seven other spirits more wicked than itself, and they go in and live there.'   MATTHEW 12:43–45

6. 'Those who have . . . those who do not have'

'Those who have will be given more, and they will have an abundance. Those who do not have, even what they have will be taken from them.'   MATTHEW 13:12

7. 'Come to a quiet place'

Then, because so many people were coming and going that they did not even have a chance to eat, he said to them, 'Come with me by yourselves to a quiet place and get some rest.'   MARK 6:31

8. What makes a person unclean

'Listen and understand. What goes into your mouth does not make you "unclean", but what comes out of your mouth, that is what makes you "unclean".'   MATTHEW 15:10

9. First and last

'Anyone who wants to be first must be the very last, and the servant of all.'   MARK 9:35

10. Jesus and little children

'Let the little children come to me, and do not hinder them, for the kingdom of heaven belongs to such as these.'   MATTHEW 19:14

11. 'My kingdom is not of this world'

'My kingdom is not of this world. If it were, my servants would fight to prevent my arrest by the Jews. But now my kingdom is from another place.'   JOHN 18:36

12. Good and evil

'Good people bring good things out of the good stored up in their hearts, and evil people bring evil things out of the evil stored up in their hearts. For out of the overflow of one's heart the mouth speaks.'   LUKE 6:45

13. Doing Jesus' will

'Not everyone who says to me, "Lord, Lord," will enter the kingdom of heaven, but only those who do the will of my Father who is in heaven. Many will say to me on that day, "Lord, Lord, did we not prophesy in your name, and in your name drive out demons and perform many miracles?" Then I will tell them plainly, "I never knew you. Away from me, you evil-doers!"'   MATTHEW 7:21–23

14. 'A cup of cold water'

'Anyone who gives you a cup of cold water in my name because you belong to Christ will certainly be rewarded.'   MARK 9:41

15. Peter's denial predicted

Immediately the cock crowed the second time. Then Peter remembered the word Jesus had spoken to him: 'Before the cock crows twice you will disown me three times.'   MARK 14:72

16. The blind leading the blind

'Can a blind man lead a blind man? Will they not both fall into a pit?' LUKE 6:39

17. Students and teachers

'A student is not above his teacher, but everyone who is fully trained will be like his teacher.' LUKE 6:40

18. 'Take the plank out of your eye'

'Why do you look at the speck of sawdust in someone else's eye and pay no attention to the plank in your own eye? How can you say, "Friend, let me take the speck out of your eye," when you yourself fail to see the plank in your own eye? You hypocrite, first take the plank out of your eye, and then you will see clearly to remove the speck from the other person's eye.' LUKE 6:41–42

19. Jesus' mother and brothers

'My mother and brothers are those who hear God's word and put it into practice.' LUKE 8:21

20. Greed

'Watch out! Be on your guard against all kinds of greed; life does not consist in the abundance of possessions.' LUKE 12:15

21. Worry

'Consider how the lilies grow. They do not labour or spin. Yet I tell you, not even Solomon in all his splendour was dressed like one of these. If that is how God clothes the grass of the field, which is here today, and tomorrow is thrown into the fire, how much more will he clothe you, O you of little faith! And do not set your heart on what you will eat or drink; do not worry about it. For the pagan world runs after all such things, and your Father knows that you need them. But seek his kingdom, and these things will be given to you as well.'   LUKE 12:27–31

22. Inviting friends round

Jesus said to his host, 'When you give a luncheon or dinner, do not invite your friends, brothers, sisters, relatives, or your rich neighbours; if you do, they may invite you back and so you will be repaid. But when you give a banquet, invite the poor, the crippled, the lame, the blind, and you will be blessed. Although they cannot repay you, you will be repaid at the resurrection of the righteous.'   LUKE 14:12–14

✌ QUESTIONS AND ANSWERS ☙

A. Questions Jesus asked

1. 'Who do you say I am?'

'Who do people say the Son of Man is?'
He [Jesus] asked his disciples, 'Who do people say the Son of Man is?'

They replied, 'Some say John the Baptist; others say Elijah; and still others, Jeremiah or one of the prophets.'

'You are the Christ'
'But what about you?' he asked. 'Who do you say I am?'

Simon Peter answered, 'You are the Christ, the Son of the living God.'

Jesus replied, 'Blessed are you, Simon son of Jonah, for this was not revealed to you by flesh and blood, but by my Father in heaven. And I tell you that you are Peter [Peter means rock], and on this rock I will build my church, and the gates of Hades will not overcome it. I will give you the keys of the kingdom of heaven; whatever you bind on earth will be bound in heaven, and whatever you loose on earth will be loosed in heaven.'
MATTHEW 16:13–19

2. 'What did you go out into the desert to see?'

As John's disciples were leaving, Jesus began to speak to the crowd about John [the Baptist]: 'What did you go out into the desert to see? A reed swayed by the wind? If not, what did you go out to see? A man dressed in fine clothes? No, those who wear fine clothes are in kings' palaces. Then what did you go out to see? A prophet? Yes, I tell you, and more than a prophet. This is the one about whom it is written:

'"I will send my messenger ahead of you,
who will prepare your way before you."
I tell you the truth: Among those born of women there has not risen anyone greater than John the Baptist; yet whoever is least in the kingdom of heaven is greater than he.'   MATTHEW 11:7–11

3. 'To what can I compare this generation?'

'To what can I compare this generation? They are like children sitting in the market-places and calling out to others:

'"We played the flute for you, and you did not dance;
we sang a dirge, and you did not mourn."
For John came neither eating nor drinking, and they say, "He has a demon." The Son of Man came eating and drinking, and they say, "Here is a glutton and a drunkard, a friend of tax

23

collectors and 'sinners'." But wisdom is proved right by her actions.'   MATTHEW 11:16–19

4. 'How can you who are evil say anything good?'

'Make a tree good and its fruit will be good, or make a tree bad and its fruit will be bad, for a tree is recognised by its fruit. You brood of vipers, how can you who are evil say anything good? For out of the overflow of the heart the mouth speaks. Good people bring good things out of the good stored up in them, and evil people bring evil things out of the evil stored up in them.

'But I tell you that people will have to give account on the day of judgment for every careless word they have spoken. For by your words you will be acquitted, and by your words you will be condemned.'   MATTHEW 12:33–37

5. 'Why are you bothering this woman?'

'Why this waste?'
While Jesus was in Bethany in the home of Simon the Leper, a woman came to him with an alabaster jar of very expensive perfume, which she poured on his head as he was reclining at the table.

When the disciples saw this, they were indignant. 'Why this waste?' they asked. 'This perfume could have been sold at a high price, and the money given to the poor.'

'She did it to prepare me for burial'
Aware of this, Jesus said to them, 'Why are you bothering this woman? She has done a beautiful thing to me. The poor you will always have with you, but you will not always have me. When she poured this perfume on my body, she did it to prepare me for burial. I tell you the truth, wherever this gospel is preached throughout the world, what she has done will also be told, in memory of her.'   MATTHEW 26:6–13

6. 'Is it lawful to heal on the Sabbath?'

A man suffering from dropsy
One Sabbath, when Jesus went to eat in the house of a prominent Pharisee, he was being carefully watched. There in front of him was a man suffering from dropsy. Jesus asked the Pharisees and experts in the law, 'Is it lawful to heal on the Sabbath or not?' But they remained silent. So taking hold of the man, he healed him and sent him away.

'What if your ox falls into a well?'
Then he asked them, 'If one of you has a son or an ox that falls into a well on the Sabbath day, will you not immediately pull it out?' And they had nothing to say.   LUKE 14:1–6

7. 'How can you say, "Show us the Father"?'

'If you really knew me . . .'
'If you really knew me, you would know my Father as well. From now on, you do know him and have seen him.'

Philip said, 'Lord, show us the Father and that will be enough for us.'

'I am in the Father, the Father is in me'
Jesus answered: 'Don't you know me, Philip, even after I have been among you such a long time? Anyone who has seen me has seen the Father. How can you say, "Show us the Father"? Don't you believe that I am in the Father, and that the Father is in me? The words I say to you are not just my own. Rather, it is the Father, living in me, who is doing his work. Believe me when I say that I am in the Father and the Father is in me; or at least believe on the evidence of the miracles themselves.

'I tell you the truth, all who have faith in me will do what I have been doing, and they will do even greater things than these, because I am going to the Father. And I will do whatever you ask in my name, so that the Son may bring glory to the

Father. You may ask me for anything in my name, and I will do it.'   JOHN 14:7–14

8. 'Simon, do you truly love me?'

'Take care of my sheep'
Jesus said to Simon Peter, 'Simon son of John, do you truly love me more than these?'

'Yes, Lord,' he said, 'you know that I love you.'

Jesus said, 'Feed my lambs.'

Again Jesus said, 'Simon son of John, do you truly love me?'

He answered, 'Yes, Lord, you know that I love you.'

Jesus said, 'Take care of my sheep.'

The third time he said to him, 'Simon son of John, do you love me?'

Peter was hurt because Jesus asked him the third time, 'Do you love me?' He said, 'Lord, you know all things; you know that I love you.'

Jesus said, 'Feed my sheep.'

Peter's martyrdom is predicted
'I tell you the truth, when you were younger you dressed yourself and went where you wanted; but when you are old you will stretch out your hands, and someone else will dress you and lead you where you do not want to go.'

Jesus said this to indicate the kind of death by which Peter would glorify God. Then he said to him, 'Follow me!'   JOHN 21:15–19

9. 'If I want him to remain alive until I return what is that to you?'

Peter turned and saw that the disciple whom Jesus loved was following them. (This was the one who had leaned back against Jesus at the supper and had said, 'Lord, who is going to betray you?') When Peter saw him, he asked, 'Lord, what about him?'

Jesus answered, 'If I want him to remain alive until I return what is that to you? You must follow me.' Because of this, the rumour spread among the believers that this disciple would not die. But Jesus did not say that he would not die; he only said, 'If I want him to remain alive until I return, what is that to you?' JOHN 21:20–23

B. The answers Jesus gave

1. 'Are only a few people going to be saved?'

'Enter through the narrow door'
Someone asked him [Jesus], 'Lord, are only a few people going to be saved?'

He said to them, 'Make every effort to enter through the narrow door, because many, I tell you, will try to enter and will not be able to. Once the owner of the house gets up and closes the door, you will stand outside knocking and pleading, "Sir, open the door for us."

'But he will answer, "I don't know you or where you come from."

'Then you will say, "We ate and drank with you, and you taught in our streets."

'But he will reply, "I don't know you or where you come from. Away from me, all you evildoers!"'

'The last will be first and the first will be last'
'There will be weeping there, and gnashing of teeth, when you see Abraham, Isaac and Jacob and all the prophets in the kingdom of God, but you yourselves thrown out. People will come from east and west and north and south, and will take their places at the feast in the kingdom of God. Indeed there are those who are last who will be first, and first who will be last.' LUKE 13:23–30

2. 'Why does your teacher eat with . . . "sinners"?'

While Jesus was having dinner at Matthew's house, many tax collectors and 'sinners' came and ate with him and his disciples. When the Pharisees saw this, they asked his disciples, 'Why does your teacher eat with tax collectors and "sinners"?'

On hearing this, Jesus said, 'It is not the healthy who need a doctor, but the sick. But go and learn what this means: "I desire mercy, not sacrifice." For I have not come to call the righteous, but sinners.'   MATTHEW 9:10–13

3. 'How is it that . . . your disciples do not fast?'

One day you will fast
Then John's disciples came and asked him [Jesus], 'How is it that we and the Pharisees fast, but your disciples do not fast?'

Jesus answered, 'How can the guests of the bridegroom mourn while he is with them? The time will come when the bridegroom will be taken from them; then they will fast.'

New wine needs new wineskins
'No-one sews a patch of unshrunk cloth on an old garment, for the patch will pull away from the garment, making the tear worse.

'Neither do people pour new wine into old wineskins. If they do, the skins will burst, the wine will run out and the wineskins will be ruined. No, they pour new wine into new wineskins, and both are preserved.'   MATTHEW 9:14–17

4. 'Are you the one who was to come?'

When John [the Baptist] heard in prison what Christ was doing, he sent his disciples to ask him, 'Are you the one who was to come, or should we expect someone else?'

Jesus replied, 'Go back and report to John what you hear and see: The blind receive sight, the lame walk, those who have leprosy are cured, the deaf hear, the dead are raised, and the good news is preached to the poor. Blessed is anyone who does not fall away on account of me.'   MATTHEW 11:2–6

5. 'Why are you doing what is unlawful on the Sabbath?'

One Sabbath Jesus was going through the cornfields, and as his disciples walked along, they began to pick some ears of corn. The Pharisees said to him, 'Look, why are they doing what is unlawful on the Sabbath?'

He answered, 'Have you never read what David did when he and his companions were hungry and in need? In the days of Abiathar the high priest, he entered the house of God and ate the consecrated bread, which is lawful only for priests to eat. And he also gave some to his companions.'

'The Sabbath was made for people'
Then he said to them, 'The Sabbath was made for people, not people for the Sabbath. So the Son of Man is Lord even of the Sabbath.'   MARK 2:23–28

6. 'Is it lawful to heal on the Sabbath?'

He [Jesus] went into their synagogue, and a man with a shrivelled hand was there. Looking for a reason to accuse Jesus, they asked him, 'Is it lawful to heal on the Sabbath?'

He said to them, 'If any of you has a sheep and it falls into a pit on the Sabbath, will you not take hold of it and lift it out? How much more valuable is a human being than a sheep! Therefore it is lawful to do good on the Sabbath.'

Then he said to the man, 'Stretch out your hand.' So he stretched it out and it was completely restored, just as sound as the other. But the Pharisees went out and plotted how they might kill Jesus.   MATTHEW 12:9–14

7. 'Why do your disciples break the tradition of the elders?'

'They don't wash their hands before they eat!'
Some Pharisees and teachers of the law came to Jesus from Jerusalem and asked, 'Why do your disciples break the tradition of the elders? They don't wash their hands before they eat!'

'You nullify the word of God for the sake of your tradition'
Jesus replied, 'And why do you break the command of God for the sake of your tradition? For God said, "Honour your father and mother" and "Anyone who curses father or mother must be put to death." But you say that if any say to their father or mother, "Whatever help you might otherwise have received from me is a gift devoted to God," they are not to "honour their father or mother" with it. Thus you nullify the word of God for the sake of your tradition. You hypocrites! Isaiah was right when he prophesied about you:

'"These people honour me with their lips,
  but their hearts are far from me.
They worship me in vain;
  their teachings are merely human rules."'   MATTHEW 15:1–9

8. 'Why then do the teachers of the law say that Elijah must come first?'

Jesus instructed them [his disciples], 'Don't tell anyone what you have seen, until the Son of Man has been raised from the dead.'

The disciples asked him, 'Why then do the teachers of the law say that Elijah must come first?'

Jesus replied, 'To be sure, Elijah comes and will restore all things. But I tell you, Elijah has already come, and they did not recognise him, but have done to him everything they wished.

In the same way the Son of Man is going to suffer at their hands.'

Then the disciples understood that he was talking to them about John the Baptist. MATTHEW 17:9–13

9. 'Why couldn't we drive it [the demon] out?'

'Your disciples could not heal him'

When they [his disciples] came to the crowd, a man approached Jesus and knelt before him. 'Lord, have mercy on my son,' he said. 'He has seizures and is suffering greatly. He often falls into the fire or into the water. I brought him to your disciples, but they could not heal him.'

'O unbelieving and perverse generation,' Jesus replied, 'how long shall I stay with you? How long shall I put up with you? Bring the boy here to me.' Jesus rebuked the demon, and it came out of the boy, and he was healed from that moment.

Then the disciples came to Jesus in private and asked, 'Why couldn't we drive it out?'

'Nothing will be impossible for you'

He replied, 'Because you have so little faith. I tell you the truth, if you have faith as small as a mustard seed, you can say to this mountain, "Move from here to there" and it will move. Nothing will be impossible for you.' MATTHEW 17:14–21

10. 'Doesn't your teacher pay the temple tax?'

The collectors of the two-drachma tax came to Peter and asked, 'Doesn't your teacher pay the temple tax?'

'Yes, he does,' he replied.

When Peter came into the house, Jesus was the first to speak. 'What do you think, Simon?' he asked. 'From whom do the kings of the earth collect duty and taxes – from their own children or from others?'

'From others,' Peter answered.

'You will find a four-drachma coin in the mouth of the fish'

'Then the children are exempt,' Jesus said to him. 'But so that we may not offend them, go to the lake and throw out your line. Take the first fish you catch; open its mouth and you will find a four-drachma coin. Take it and give it to them for my tax and yours.'   MATTHEW 17:24–32

11. 'Who is the greatest in the kingdom of heaven?'

The disciples came to Jesus and asked, 'Who is the greatest in the kingdom of heaven?'

He called a little child whom he placed among them. And he said, 'I tell you the truth, unless you change and become like little children, you will never enter the kingdom of heaven. Therefore, those who humble themselves like this child are the greatest in the kingdom of heaven.'

'And whoever welcomes a little child like this in my name welcomes me.'   MATTHEW 18:1–5

12. 'How many times shall I forgive someone?'

'Not seven times, but seventy-seven times'

Peter came to Jesus and asked, 'Lord, how many times shall I forgive someone who sins against me? Up to seven times?'

Jesus answered, 'I tell you, not seven times, but seventy-seven times.'

The ten-thousand-talent debt

'Therefore, the kingdom of heaven is like a king who wanted to settle accounts with his servants. As he began the settlement, a man who owed him ten thousand talents was brought to him. Since he was not able to pay, the master ordered that he and his wife and his children and all that he had be sold to repay the debt.

'The servant fell on his knees before him, "Be patient with

32

me," he begged, "and I will pay back everything." The servant's master took pity on him, cancelled the debt and let him go.'

The one-hundred-denarii debt

'But when that servant went out, he found one of his fellow-servants who owed him a hundred denarii. He grabbed him and began to choke him. "Pay back what you owe me!" he demanded.

'His fellow-servant fell to his knees and begged him, "Be patient with me, and I will pay you back.'

But he refused. Instead, he went off and had the man thrown into prison until he could pay the debt. When the other servants saw what had happened, they were greatly distressed and went and told their master everything that had happened.

'Then the master called the servant in. "You wicked servant," he said, "I cancelled all that debt of yours because you begged me to. Shouldn't you have had mercy on your fellow-servant just as I had on you?" In anger his master turned him over to the jailers to be tortured, until he should pay back all he owed.

'This is how my heavenly Father will treat each of you unless you forgive one another from your heart.' MATTHEW 18:21-35

13. 'Is it lawful for a man to divorce his wife?'

Some Pharisees came to him [Jesus] to test him. They asked, 'Is it lawful for a man to divorce his wife for any and every reason?'

'Haven't you read,' he replied, 'that at the beginning the Creator "made them male and female", and said, "For this reason a man will leave his father and mother and be united to his wife, and the two will become one flesh"?'

'What God has joined together, let no-one separate'

'So they are no longer two, but one. Therefore what God has joined together, let no-one separate.'

'Why then,' they asked, 'did Moses command that a man give his wife a certificate of divorce and send her away?'

Jesus replied, 'Moses permitted you to divorce your wives because your hearts were hard. But it was not this way from the beginning. I tell you that anyone who divorces his wife, except for marital unfaithfulness, and marries another woman commits adultery.'   MATTHEW 19:3–9

14. Is it better never to marry?

The disciples said to him [Jesus], 'If this is the situation between a husband and wife, it is better not to marry.'

Jesus replied, 'Not everyone can accept this word, but only those to whom it has been given. For some are eunuchs because they were born that way; others have been made that way; and others have renounced marriage because of the kingdom of heaven. The one who can accept this should accept it.'   MATTHEW 19:10–12

15. 'Who can be saved?'

The disciples were even more amazed, and said to each other, 'Who then can be saved?'

Jesus looked at them and said, 'Humanly, this is impossible, but not with God; all things are possible with God.'   MARK 10:26–27

16. 'By what authority are you doing these things?'

The chief priests and the elders of the people came to him [Jesus]. 'By what authority are you doing these things?' they asked. 'And who gave you this authority?'

Jesus replied, 'I will also ask you one question. If you answer me, I will tell you by what authority I am doing these things. John's baptism – where did it come from? Was it from heaven, or of human origin?'

They discussed it among themselves and said, 'If we say, "From heaven", he will ask, "Then why didn't you believe him?" But if we say, "Of human origin" – we are afraid of the people, for they all hold that John was a prophet.'

So they answered Jesus, 'We don't know.'

Then he said, 'Neither will I tell you by what authority I am doing these things.'   MATTHEW 21:23–27

17. 'Is it right for us to pay taxes to Caesar or not?'

Keeping a close watch on him, they sent spies, who pretended to be honest. They hoped to catch Jesus in something he said so that they might hand him over to the power and authority of the governor. So the spies questioned him: 'Teacher, we know that you speak and teach what is right, and that you do not show partiality but teach the way of God in accordance with the truth. Is it right for us to pay taxes to Caesar or not?'

'Give to Caesar what is Caesar's, and to God what is God's'

He saw through their duplicity and said to them, 'Show me a denarius. Whose portrait and inscription are on it?'

'Caesar's,' they replied.

He said to them, 'Then give to Caesar what is Caesar's, and to God what is God's.'

They were unable to trap him in what he had said there in public. And astonished by his answer, they became silent.
LUKE 20:20–26

18. 'Why don't your disciples fast?'

They said to him, 'John's disciples often fast and pray, and so do the disciples of the Pharisees, but yours go on eating and drinking.'

Jesus answered, 'Can you make the guests of the bridegroom

fast while he is with them? But the time will come when the bridegroom will be taken from them; in those days they will fast.'

He told them this parable: 'No-one tears a patch from a new garment and sews it on an old one. Whoever does will have torn the new garment, and the patch from the new will not match the old. And no-one pours new wine into old wineskins. If anyone does, the new wine will burst the skins, the wine will run out and the wineskins will be ruined. No, new wine must be poured into new wineskins. And none of you, after drinking old wine, wants the new, for you say, "The old is better."' LUKE 5:33–39

19. 'When will the kingdom of God come?'

Once, having been asked by the Pharisees when the kingdom of God would come, Jesus replied, 'The kingdom of God does not come with your careful observation, nor will people say, "Here it is," or "There it is," because the kingdom of God is within you.' LUKE 17:20–21

20. 'What must we do to do the work God requires?'

'What must we do to do the works God requires?'

Jesus answered, 'The work of God is this: to believe in the one he has sent.' JOHN 6:28–29

21. 'What miraculous sign will you do?'

So they asked him, 'What miraculous sign then will you give that we may see it and believe you? What will you do? Our ancestors ate the manna in the desert; as it is written: "He gave them bread from heaven to eat."'

Jesus said to them, 'I tell you the truth, it is not Moses who has given you the bread from heaven, but it is my Father who gives you the true bread from heaven. For the bread of God is he who comes down from heaven and gives life to the world.'

'Sir,' they said, 'from now on give us this bread.'   JOHN 6:30-34

22. 'How does this man get so much learning without having studied?'

Not until halfway through the Feast did Jesus go up to the temple courts and begin to teach. The Jews were amazed and asked, 'How did this man get such learning without having studied?'

'My teaching is not my own'

Jesus answered, 'My teaching is not my own. It comes from him who sent me. Anyone who chooses to do the will of God will find out whether my teaching comes from God or whether I speak on my own. Those who speak on their own do so to gain honour for themselves, but he who works for the honour of the one who sent him is a man of truth; there is nothing false about him. Has not Moses given you the law? Yet not one of you keeps the law. Why are you trying to kill me?'   JOHN 7:14-19

23. 'Who is trying to kill you?'

'You are demon-possessed,' the crowd answered. 'Who is trying to kill you?'

Jesus said to them, 'I did one miracle, and you are all astonished. Yet, because Moses gave you circumcision (though actually it did not come from Moses, but from the patriarchs), you circumcise a child on the Sabbath. Now if a child can be circumcised on the Sabbath so that the law of Moses may not be broken, why are you angry with me for healing the whole person on the Sabbath? Stop judging by mere appearances, and make a right judgment.'   JOHN 7:20-24

24. Is Jesus the Christ?

At that point some of the people of Jerusalem began to ask, 'Isn't this the man they are trying to kill? Here he is, speaking publicly, and they are not saying a word to him. Have the authorities really concluded that he is the Christ? But we know where this man is from; when the Christ comes, no-one will know where he is from.'

Then Jesus, still teaching in the temple courts, cried out, 'Yes, you know me, and you know where I am from. I am not here on my own, but he who sent me is true. You do not know him, but I know him because I am from him and he sent me.'

JOHN 7:25–29

25. 'Where does this man intend to go that we cannot find him?'

'I am with you for only a short time'
Jesus said, 'I am with you for only a short time, and then I go to the one who sent me. You will look for me, but you will not find me; and where I am, you cannot come.'

The Jews said to one another, 'Where does this man intend to go that we cannot find him? Will he go where our people live scattered among the Greeks, and teach the Greeks? What did he mean when he said, "You will look for me, but you will not find me," and "Where I am you cannot come"?'

JOHN 7:33–36

26. 'How can you say that we shall be set free?'

'Everyone who sins is a slave to sin'
To the Jews who had believed him, Jesus said, 'If you hold to my teaching, you are really my disciples. Then you will know the truth, and the truth will set you free.'

They answered him, 'We are Abraham's descendants and

have never been slaves of anyone. How can you say that we shall be set free?'

Jesus replied, 'I tell you the truth, everyone who sins is a slave to sin. Now a slave has no permanent place in the family, but a son belongs to it for ever. So if the Son sets you free, you will be free indeed. I know you are Abraham's descendants. Yet you are ready to kill me, because you have no room for my word. I am telling you what I have seen in the Father's presence, and you do what you have heard from your father.'

'Abraham is our father,' they answered.

'If you were Abraham's children,' said Jesus, 'then you would do the things Abraham did. As it is, you are determined to kill me, a man who has told you the truth that I heard from God. Abraham did not do such things. You are doing the things your own father does.'

'We are not illegitimate children,' they protested. 'The only Father we have is God himself.'

'If God were your Father, you would love me'
Jesus said to them, 'If God were your Father, you would love me, for I came from God and now am here. I have not come on my own; but he sent me. Why is my language not clear to you? Because you are unable to hear what I say. You belong to your father, the devil, and you want to carry out your father's desire. He was a murderer from the beginning, not holding to the truth, for there is no truth in him. When he lies, he speaks his native language, for he is a liar and the father of lies. Yet because I tell the truth, you do not believe me! Can any of you prove me guilty of sin? If I am telling the truth, why don't you believe me? Whoever belongs to God hears what God says. The reason you do not hear is that you do not belong to God.' JOHN 8:31–47

27. 'Aren't we right in saying that you are demon-possessed?'

'Whoever keeps my word will never see death'

The Jews answered him, 'Aren't we right in saying that you are a Samaritan and demon-possessed?'

'I am not possessed by a demon,' said Jesus, 'but I honour my Father and you dishonour me. I am not seeking glory for myself; but there is one who seeks it, and he is the judge. I tell you the truth, whoever keeps my word will never see death.'

At this the Jews exclaimed, 'Now we know that you are demon-possessed! Abraham died and so did the prophets, yet you say that whoever keeps your word will never taste death. Are you greater than our father Abraham? He died, and so did the prophets. Who do you think you are?'

'Before Abraham was born, I am!'

Jesus replied, 'If I glorify myself, my glory means nothing. My Father, whom you claim as your God, is the one who glorifies me. Though you do not know him, I know him. If I said I did not, I would be a liar like you, but I do know him and keep his word. Your father Abraham rejoiced at the thought of seeing my day; he saw it and was glad.'

'You are not yet fifty years old,' the Jews said to him, 'and you have seen Abraham!'

'I tell you the truth,' Jesus answered, 'before Abraham was born, I am!' At this, they picked up stones to stone him, but Jesus hid himself, slipping away from the temple grounds.
JOHN 8:48–59

28. 'How long will you keep us in suspense?'

'I and the Father are one'

Then came the Feast of Dedication at Jerusalem. It was winter, and Jesus was in the temple area walking in Solomon's Colonnade. The Jews gathered round him, saying, 'How long will you keep us in suspense? If you are the Christ, tell us plainly.'

Jesus answered, 'I did tell you, but you do not believe. The miracles I do in my Father's name speak for me, but you do not believe because you are not my sheep. My sheep listen to my voice; I know them, and they follow me. I give them eternal life, and they shall never perish; no-one can snatch them out of my hand. My Father, who has given them to me, is greater than all; no-one can snatch them out of my Father's hand. I and the Father are one.'

Again the Jews picked up stones to stone him, but Jesus said to them, 'I have shown you many great miracles from the Father. For which of these do you stone me?'

'We are not stoning you for any of these,' replied the Jews, 'but for blasphemy, because you, a mere human being, claim to be God.'

'Believe in the miracles'

Jesus answered them, 'Is it not written in your Law, "I have said you are gods"? If he called them "gods", to whom the word of God came – and the Scripture cannot be broken – what about the one whom the Father set apart as his very own and sent into the world? Why then do you accuse me of blasphemy because I said "I am God's Son"? Do not believe me unless I do what my Father does. But if I do it, even though you do not believe me, believe the miracles, that you may learn and understand that the Father is in me, and I in the Father.' Again they tried to seize him, but he escaped their grasp.   JOHN 10:22–39

29. 'What does he mean by "a little while"?'

'In a little while you will see me no more, and then after a little while you will see me.'

'You will weep and mourn'

Some of his disciples said to one another, 'What does he mean by saying, "In a little while you will see me no more, and then after a little while you will see me," and "Because I am going to the Father"?' They kept asking, 'What does he mean by "a little while"? We don't understand what he is saying.'

Jesus saw that they wanted to ask him about this, so he said to them, 'Are you asking one another what I meant when I said, "In a little while you will see me no more, and then after a little while you will see me"?'

'I will see you again'

'I tell you the truth, you will weep and mourn while the world rejoices. You will grieve, but your grief will turn to joy. A woman giving birth to a child has pain because her time has come; but when her baby is born she forgets the anguish because of her joy that a child is born into the world. So with you: Now is your time of grief, but I will see you again and you will rejoice, and no-one will take away your joy.'   JOHN 16:16–22

✥ THE PEOPLE JESUS MET ✥

A. The twelve disciples

1. Four fishermen

Simon Peter and Andrew

As Jesus walking beside the Sea of Galilee, he saw two brothers, Simon called Peter and his brother Andrew. They were casting a net into the lake, for they were fishermen. 'Come, follow me,' Jesus said, 'and I will make you fishers of men and women.' At once they left their nets and followed him.

James and John

Going on from there, he saw two other brothers, James son of Zebedee and his brother John. They were in a boat with their father Zebedee, preparing their nets. Jesus called them,

and immediately they left the boat and their father and
followed him.   MATTHEW 4:18–22

2. Philip and Nathanael are called

'Follow me'
The next day Jesus decided to leave for Galilee. Finding Philip,
he said to him, 'Follow me.'

Philip, like Andrew and Peter, was from the town of
Bethsaida. Philip found Nathanael and told him, 'We have
found the one Moses wrote about in the Law, and about whom
the prophets also wrote – Jesus of Nazareth, the son of Joseph.'

'Nazareth! Can anything good come from there?' Nathanael
asked.

'Come and see,' said Philip.

'You shall see heaven open'
When Jesus saw Nathanael approaching, he said of him, 'Here
is a true Israelite, in whom there is nothing false.'

'How do you know me?' Nathanael asked.

Jesus answered, 'I saw you while you were still under the fig-
tree before Philip called you.'

Then Nathanael declared, 'Rabbi, you are the Son of God;
you are the King of Israel.'

Jesus said, 'You believe because I told you I saw you under
the fig-tree. You shall see greater things than that.' He then
added, 'I tell you the truth, you shall see heaven open, and the
angels of God ascending and descending on the Son of
Man.'   JOHN 1:43–51

3. Matthew (Levi) is called

Jesus went out and saw a tax collector by the name of Levi sitting at his tax booth. 'Follow me,' Jesus said to him, and Levi
got up, left everything and followed him.   LUKE 5:27–28

B. The Pharisees

1. Jesus is linked to Beelzebub

Then they brought him a demon-possessed man who was blind and mute, and Jesus healed him, so that he could both talk and see. All the people were astonished and said, 'Could this be the Son of David?'

But when the Pharisees heard this, they said, 'It is only by Beelzebub, the prince of demons, that this fellow drives out demons.'

Jesus knew their thoughts and said to them, 'Every kingdom divided against itself will be ruined, and every city or household divided against itself will not stand. If Satan drives out Satan, he is divided against himself. How then can his kingdom stand? And if I drive out demons by Beelzebub, by whom do your people drive them out? So then, they will be your judges. But if I drive out demons by the spirit of God, then the kingdom of God has come upon you.   MATTHEW 12:22–28

2. 'Whose son is the Christ?'

While the Pharisees were gathered together, Jesus asked them, 'What do you think about the Christ? Whose son is he?'

'The son of David,' they replied.

He said to them, 'How is it then that David, speaking by the Spirit, calls him "Lord"? For he says,

'"The Lord said to my Lord:
   'Sit at my right hand
until I put your enemies
   under your feet."'

If then David calls him "Lord", how can he be his son?' No-one could say a word in reply, and from that day on no-one dared to ask him any more questions.   MATTHEW 22:41–46

3. The Pharisees and Herod

At that time some Pharisees came to Jesus and said to him, 'Leave this place and go somewhere else. Herod wants to kill you.'

He replied, 'Go tell that fox, "I will drive out demons and heal people today and tomorrow, and on the third day I will reach my goal." In any case, I must keep going today and tomorrow and the next day – for surely no prophet can die outside Jerusalem!

'O Jerusalem, Jerusalem, you who kill the prophets and stone those sent to you, how often have I longed to gather your children together, as hen gathers her chicks under her wings, but you were not willing! Look, your house is left to you desolate. I tell you, you will not see me again until you say, "Blessed is he who comes in the name of the Lord."'　LUKE 13:31–35

4. At the house of Simon the Pharisee

A woman who had lived a sinful life . . .

Now one of the Pharisees invited Jesus to have dinner with him, so he went to the Pharisee's house and reclined at the table. When a woman who had lived a sinful life in that town learned that Jesus was eating at the Pharisee's house, she brought an alabaster jar of perfume, and as she stood behind him at his feet weeping, she began to wet his feet with her tears. Then she wiped them with her hair, kissed them and poured perfume on them.

When the Pharisee who had invited him saw this, he said to himself, 'If this man were a prophet, he would know who is touching him and what kind of woman she is – that she is a sinner.'

'He who has been forgiven little loves little'

Jesus answered him, 'Simon, I have something to tell you.'

'Tell me, teacher,' he said.

'Two men owed money to a certain money-lender. One owed him five hundred denarii, and the other fifty. Neither of them had the money to pay him back, so he cancelled the debts of both. Now which of them will love him more?'

Simon replied, 'I suppose the one who had the bigger debt cancelled.'

'You have judged correctly,' Jesus said.

Then he turned towards the woman and said to Simon, 'Do you see this woman? I came into your house. You did not give me any water for my feet, but she wet my feet with her tears and wiped them with her hair. You did not give me a kiss, but this woman, from the time I entered, has not stopped kissing my feet. You did not put oil on my head, but she has poured perfume on my feet. Therefore, I tell you, her many sins have been forgiven – for she loved much. But the one who has been forgiven little loves little.'

'Your faith has saved you; go in peace'
Then Jesus said to her, 'Your sins are forgiven.'

The other guests began to say among themselves, 'Who is this who even forgives sins?'

Jesus said to the woman, 'Your faith has saved you; go in peace.' LUKE 7:36–50

5. The Pharisees sneer at Jesus

The Pharisees, who loved money, heard all this and were sneering at Jesus. He said to them, 'You are the ones who justify yourselves in the eyes of others, but God knows your hearts. What is highly valued by people is detestable in God's sight.

'The Law and the Prophet were proclaimed until John. Since that time, the good news of the kingdom of God is being preached, and people are forcing their way into it. It is easier for heaven and earth to disappear than for the least stroke of a pen to drop out of the Law.' LUKE 16:14–17

C. The teachers of the law and the Sadducees

1. They demand a miracle

Then some of the Pharisees and teachers of the law said to him, 'Teacher, we want see a miraculous sign from you.'

He answered, 'A wicked and adulterous generation asks for a miraculous sign! But none will be given it except the sign of the prophet Jonah. For as Jonah was three days and three nights in the belly of a huge fish, so the Son of Man will be three days and three nights in the heart of the earth. The men of Nineveh will stand up at the judgment with this generation and condemn it; for they repented at the preaching of Jonah, and now one greater than Jonah is here. The Queen of the South will rise at the judgment with this generation and condemn it; for she came from the ends of the earth to listen to Solomon's wisdom, and now one greater than Solomon is here.'   MATTHEW 12:38–42

2. Jesus warns against the teachers of the law

'They tie heavy loads and put them on other people's shoulders'
Then Jesus said to the crowds and to his disciples: 'The teachers of the law and the Pharisees sit in Moses' seat. So you must obey them and do everything they tell you. But do not do what they do, for they do not practise what they preach. They tie up heavy loads and put them on other people's shoulders, but they themselves are not willing to lift a finger to move them.'

'They make their phylacteries wide'
'Everything they do is done for others to see: They make their phylacteries wide and the tassels on their garments long; they love the place of honour at banquets and the most important seats in the synagogues; they love to be greeted in the market-places and to have people call them "Rabbi".

'The greatest among you will be your servant'

'But you are not to be called "Rabbi", for you have only one master and you are all brothers and sisters. And do not call anyone on earth "father", for you have one Father, and he is in heaven. Nor are you to be called "teacher", for you have one Teacher, the Christ. The greatest among you will be your servant. For those who exalt themselves will be humbled, and those who humble themselves will be exalted.'   MATTHEW 23:1–12

3. Seven woes against the teachers of the law

'Woe to you for shutting the kingdom of heaven in people's faces'

'Woe to you, teachers of the law and Pharisees, you hypocrites! You shut the kingdom of heaven in people's faces. You yourselves do not enter, nor will you let those enter who are trying to.'

'Woe to you who win a convert'

'Woe to you, teachers of the law and Pharisees, you hypocrites! You travel over land and sea to win a single convert, and then you make that convert twice as much a child of hell as you are.'

'Woe to you, blind guides!'

'Woe to you, blind guides! You say, "If anyone swears by the temple, it means nothing; but whoever swears by the gold of the temple is bound by the oath." You blind fools! Which is greater: the gold, or the temple that makes the gold sacred? You also say, "If anyone swears by the altar, it means nothing; but if anyone swears by the gift on it, he is bound by his oath." You blind men! Which is greater: the gift, or the altar that makes the gift sacred? Therefore, anyone who swears by the altar swears by it and by everything on it. And anyone who swears by the temple swears by it and by the one who dwells in it. And anyone who swears by heaven swears by God's throne and by the one who sits on it.'

'Woe to you for neglecting justice and mercy'

'Woe to you, teachers of the law and Pharisees, you hypocrites! You give a tenth of your spices – mint, dill and cummin. But you have neglected the more important matters of the law – justice, mercy and faithfulness. You should have practised the latter, without neglecting the former. You blind guides! You strain out a gnat but swallow a camel.'

'Woe to you for being full of greed'

'Woe to you, teachers of the law and Pharisees, you hypocrites! You clean the outside of the cup and dish, but inside they are full of greed and self-indulgence. Blind Pharisee! First clean the inside of the cup and dish, and then the outside also will be clean.'

'Woe to you for being full of hypocrisy'

'Woe to you, teachers of the law and Pharisees, you hypocrites! You are like whitewashed tombs, which look beautiful on the outside but on the inside are full of the bones of the dead and everything unclean. In the same way, on the outside you appear to people as righteous but on the inside you are full of hypocrisy and wickedness.

'Woe to you, teachers of the law and Pharisees, you hypocrites! You build tombs for the prophets and decorate the graves of the righteous. And you say, "If we had lived in the days of our forefathers, we would not have taken part with them in shedding the blood of the prophets." So you testify against yourselves that you are the descendants of those who murdered the prophets. Fill up, then, the measure of the sin of your ancestors!'

'You snakes! You brood of vipers'

'You snakes! You brood of vipers! How will you escape being condemned to hell? Therefore I am sending you prophets and sages and teachers. Some of them you will kill and crucify; others you will flog in your synagogues and pursue from town to town. And so upon you will come all the righteous blood that has been shed on earth, from the blood of righteous Abel to the blood of Zechariah son of Barakiah, whom you murdered between the temple and the altar. I tell you the truth, all this will come upon this generation.'   MATTHEW 23:13–36

4. Jesus refuses to give a sign

The Pharisees and Sadducees came to Jesus and tested him by asking him to show them a sign from heaven.

He replied, 'When evening comes, you say, "It will be fair weather, for the sky is red," and in the morning, "Today it will be stormy, for the sky is red and overcast." You know how to interpret the appearance of the sky, but you cannot interpret the signs of the times. A wicked and adulterous generation looks for a miraculous sign, but none will be given it except the sign of Jonah.' Jesus then left them and went away.   MATTHEW 16:1–4

5. 'Be on your guard against their teaching'

When they went across the lake, the disciples forgot to take bread. 'Be careful,' Jesus said to them. 'Be on your guard against the yeast of the Pharisees and Sadducees.'

They discussed this among themselves and said, 'It is because we didn't bring any bread.'

Aware of their discussion, Jesus asked, 'You of little faith, why are you talking among yourselves about having no bread? Do you still not understand? Don't you remember the five loaves for the five thousand, and how many basketfuls you gathered? Or the seven loaves for the four thousand, and how many basketfuls you gathered? How is it you don't understand that I was not talking to you about bread? But be on your guard against the yeast of the Pharisees and Sadducees.' Then they understood that he was not telling them to guard against the yeast used in bread, but against the teaching of the Pharisees and Sadducees.   MATTHEW 16:5–12

6. A question about rising from death

That same day the Sadducees, who say there is no resurrection, came to him with a question. 'Teacher,' they said, 'Moses told us that if a man dies without having children, his brother must marry the widow and have children for him. Now there were seven brothers among us. The first one married and died, and since he had no children, he left his wife to his brother. The same thing happened to the second and third brother, right on down to the seventh. Finally, the woman died. Now then, at the resurrection, whose wife will she be of the seven, since all of them were married to her?'

'You do not know the Scriptures or the power of God'
Jesus replied, 'You are in error because you do not know the Scriptures or the power of God. At the resurrection people will neither marry nor be given in marriage; they will be like the angels in heaven. But about the resurrection of the dead – have you not read what God said to you, "I am the God of Abraham, the God of Isaac, and the God of Jacob"? He is not the God of the dead but of the living.'

When the crowds heard this, they were astonished at his teaching.   MATTHEW 22:23-33

7. 'Which is the greatest commandment in the law?'

One of the teachers of the law came and heard them debating. Noticing that Jesus had given them a good answer, he asked him, 'Of all the commandments, which is the most important?'

'Love God, love your neighbour'
'The most important one,' answered Jesus, 'is this: "Hear, O Israel, the Lord our God, the Lord is one. Love the Lord your God with all your heart and with all your soul and with all your mind and with all your strength." The second is this: "Love

your neighbour as yourself." There is no commandment greater than these.'

'Well said, teacher,' the man replied. 'You are right in saying that God is one and there is no other but him. To love him with all your heart, with all your understanding and with all your strength, and to love your neighbour as yourself is more important than all burnt offerings and sacrifices.'

'You are not far from the kingdom of God'
When Jesus saw that he had answered wisely, he said to him, 'You are not far from the kingdom of God.' And from then on no-one dared ask him any more questions.   MARK 12:28–34

D. The Jews

1. Jesus claims equality with God

'Whatever the Father does the Son also does'
For this reason the Jews tried all the harder to kill him; not only was he breaking the Sabbath, but he was even calling God his own Father, making himself equal with God.

Jesus gave them this answer: 'I tell you the truth, the Son can do nothing by himself; he can do only what he sees his Father doing, because whatever the Father does the Son also does. For the Father loves the Son and shows him all he does. Yes, to your amazement he will show him even greater things than these. For just as the Father raises the dead and gives them life, even so the Son gives life to whom he is pleased to give it. Moreover, the Father judges no-one, but has entrusted all judgment to the Son, that all may honour the Son just as they honour the Father. Whoever does not honour the Son does not honour the Father, who sent him.'

'The Father has given the Son authority to judge'

'I tell you the truth, those who hear my word and believe him who sent me has eternal life and will not be condemned; they have crossed over from death to life. I tell you the truth, a time is coming and has now come when the dead will hear the voice of the Son of God and those who hear will live. For as the Father has life in himself, so he has granted the Son to have life in himself. And he has given him authority to judge because he is the Son of Man.

'Do not be amazed at this, for a time is coming when all who are in their graves will hear his voice and come out – those who have done good will rise to live, and those who have done evil will rise to be condemned. By myself I can do nothing; I judge only as I hear, and my judgment is just, for I seek not to please myself but him who sent me.'   JOHN 5:18–30

2. Witnesses to Jesus

The witness of John the Baptist

'You have sent to John and he has testified to the truth. Not that I accept human testimony; but I mention it that you may be saved. John was a lamp that burned and gave light, and you chose for a time to enjoy his light.'

The witness of Jesus' deeds

'I have testimony weightier than that of John. For the very work that the Father has given me to finish, and which I am doing, testifies that the Father has sent me.'

The witness of the Father

'And the Father who sent me has himself testified concerning me. You have never heard his voice nor seen his form, nor does his word dwell in you, for you do not believe the one he sent.'

The witness of the Scriptures

'You diligently study the Scriptures because you think that by them you possess eternal life. These are the Scriptures that testify about me, yet you refuse to come to me to have life.

'I do not accept human praise, but I know you. I know that you do not have the love of God in your hearts. I have come in my Father's name, and you do not accept me; but if others come in their own names, you will accept them. How can you believe if you accept praise from one another, yet make no effort to obtain the praise that comes from the only God?

'But do not think I will accuse you before the Father. Your accuser is Moses, on whom your hopes are set. If you believed Moses, you would believe me, for he wrote about me. But since you do not believe what he wrote, how are you going to believe what I say?' JOHN 5:33–47

3. 'Is not this the son of Joseph?'

At this the Jews began to grumble about him because he said, 'I am the bread that came down from heaven.' They said, 'Is this not Jesus, the son of Joseph, whose father and mother we know? How can he now say, "I came down from heaven"?'

'Whoever believes has everlasting life'

'Stop grumbling among yourselves,' Jesus answered. 'No-one can come to me unless the Father who sent me draws them, and I will raise them up at the last day. It is written in the Prophets: "They will all be taught by God." Everyone who listens to the Father and learns from him comes to me. No-one has seen the Father except the one who is from God; only he has seen the Father. I tell you the truth, whoever believes has everlasting life. I am the bread of life. Your ancestors ate the manna in the desert, yet they died. But here is the bread that comes down from heaven, which people may eat and not die. I am the living bread that came down from heaven. Whoever eats of this bread will live for ever. This bread is my flesh, which I will give for the life of the world.' JOHN 6:41–51

4. 'How can this man give us his flesh to eat?'

Then the Jews began to argue sharply among themselves, 'How can this man give us his flesh to eat?'

'Those who eat my flesh have eternal life'
Jesus said to them, 'I tell you the truth, unless you eat the flesh of the Son of Man and drink his blood, you have no life in you. Those who eat my flesh and drink my blood have eternal life, and I will raise them up at the last day. For my flesh is real food and my blood is real drink. Those who eat my flesh and drink my blood remain in me, and I in them. Just as the living Father sent me and I live because of the Father, so the one who feeds on me will live because of me. This is the bread that came down from heaven. Your ancestors ate manna and died, but whoever feeds on this bread will live for ever.'   JOHN 6:52–58

'This is a hard saying'
On hearing it, many of his disciples said, 'This is a hard teaching. Who can accept it?'

Aware that his disciples were grumbling about this, Jesus said to them, 'Does this offend you? What if you see the Son of Man ascend to where he was before!'

'The Spirit gives life; the flesh counts for nothing'
'The Spirit gives life; the flesh counts for nothing. The words I have spoken to you are spirit and they are life. Yet there are some of you who do not believe.'

For Jesus had known from the beginning which of them did not believe and who would betray him. He went on to say, 'This is why I told you that no-one can come to me unless the Father has enabled them.'   JOHN 6:52–65

E. Strangers

1. A woman with faith

Leaving that place, Jesus withdrew to the region of Tyre and Sidon. A Canaanite woman from that vicinity came to him, crying out, 'Lord, Son of David, have mercy on me! My daughter is suffering terribly from demon-possession.'

Jesus did not answer a word. So his disciples came to him and urged him, 'Send her away, for she keeps crying out after us.'

He answered, 'I was sent only to the lost sheep of Israel.'

The woman came and knelt before him, 'Lord, help me!' she said.

He replied, 'It is not right to take the children's bread and toss it to their dogs.'

'Woman, you have great faith!'

'Yes, Lord,' she said, 'but even the dogs eat the crumbs that fall from their masters' table.'

Then Jesus answered, 'Woman, you have great faith! Your request is granted.' And her daughter was healed from that very hour.   MATTHEW 15:21–28

2. A rich young man

As Jesus started on his way, someone ran up to him and fell on his knees before him. 'Good teacher,' he asked, 'what must I do to inherit eternal life?'

'Why do you call me good?' Jesus answered. 'No-one is good – except God alone. You know the commandments: "Do not murder, do not commit adultery, do not steal, do not give false testimony, do not defraud, honour your father and mother."'

'Teacher,' he declared, 'all these I have kept since I was a boy.'

Jesus looked at him and loved him. 'One thing you lack,' he said. 'Go, sell everything you have and give to the poor, and you will have treasure in heaven. Then come, follow me.'

At this the man's face fell. He went away sad, because he had great wealth.   MARK 10:17–22

3. Zacchaeus

Jesus entered Jericho and was passing through. A man was there by the name of Zacchaeus; he was a chief tax collector and was wealthy. He wanted to see who Jesus was, but being a short man he could not, because of the crowd. So he ran ahead and climbed a sycamore-fig tree to see him, since Jesus was coming that way.

When Jesus reached the spot, he looked up and said to him, 'Zacchaeus, come down immediately. I must stay at your house today.' So he came down at once and welcomed him gladly.

All the people saw this and began to mutter, 'He has gone to be the guest of a "sinner".'

'I give half of my possessions to the poor'
But Zacchaeus stood up and said to the Lord, 'Look, Lord! Here and now I give half of my possessions to the poor, and if I have cheated anybody out of anything, I will pay back four times the amount.'

Jesus said to him, 'Today salvation has come to this house, because this man, too, is a son of Abraham. For the Son of Man came to seek and to save what was lost.'   LUKE 19:1–10

4. Nicodemus, a top religious leader

He came to Jesus by night
Now there was a man of the Pharisees named Nicodemus, a member of the Jewish ruling council. He came to Jesus at

night and said, 'Rabbi, we know you are a teacher who has come from God. For you could not perform the miraculous signs you are doing if God were not with you.'

In reply Jesus declared, 'I tell you the truth, no-one can see the kingdom of God without being born again.'

'How can anyone be born in old age?' Nicodemus asked. 'Surely they cannot enter a second time into their mother's womb to be born!'

'You must be born again'

Jesus answered, 'I tell you the truth, no-one can enter the kingdom of God without being born of water and the Spirit. Flesh gives birth to flesh, but the Spirit gives birth to spirit. You should not be surprised at my saying, "You must be born again." The wind blows wherever it pleases. You hear its sound, but you cannot tell where it comes from or where it is going. So it is with everyone born of the Spirit.'

'How can this be?' Nicodemus asked.

'You are Israel's teacher,' said Jesus, 'and do you not understand these things? I tell you the truth, we speak of what we know, and we testify to what we have seen, but still you people do not accept our testimony. I have spoken to you of earthly things and you do not believe; how then will you believe if I speak of heavenly things? No-one has ever gone into heaven except the one who came from heaven – the Son of Man. Just as Moses lifted up the snake in the desert, so the Son of Man must be lifted up, that everyone who believes in him may have eternal life.'

'Light has come into the world'

'For God so loved the world that he gave his one and only Son, that whoever believes in him shall not perish but have eternal life. For God did not send his Son into the world to condemn the world, but to save the world through him. Those who believe in him are not condemned, but those who do not believe stand condemned already because they have not believed in the name of God's one and only Son. This is the verdict: Light has come into the world, but people loved darkness instead of light because their deeds were evil. All those who do evil hate the light, and will not come into the light for fear that their deeds will be exposed. But those who live by the truth come into the light, so that it may be seen plainly that what they have done has been done through God.'   JOHN 3:1–21

5. A Samaritan woman

When a Samaritan woman came to draw water, Jesus said to her, 'Will you give me a drink?' (His disciples had gone into the town to buy food.)

The Samaritan woman said to him, 'You are a Jew and I am a Samaritan woman. How can you ask me for a drink?' (For Jews do not associate with Samaritans.)

Jesus answered her, 'If you knew the gift of God and who it is that asks you for a drink, you would have asked him and he would have given you living water.'

'Sir,' the woman said, 'you have nothing to draw with and the well is deep. Where can you get this living water? Are you greater than our father Jacob, who gave us the well and drank from it himself, as did also his sons and his flocks and herds?'

'Those who drink the water I give them will never thirst'
Jesus answered, 'All who drink this water will be thirsty again, but those who drink the water I give them will never thirst. Indeed, the water I give them will become in them a spring of water welling up to eternal life.'

The woman said to him, 'Sir, give me this water so that I won't get thirsty and have to keep coming here to draw water.'

He told her, 'Go, call your husband and come back.'

'I have no husband,' she replied.

Jesus said to her, 'You are right when you say you have no husband. The fact is, you have had five husbands, and the man you now have is not your husband. What you have just said is quite true.'

'Sir,' the woman said, 'I can see that you are a prophet. Our ancestors worshipped on this mountain, but you Jews claim that the place where we must worship is in Jerusalem.'

'Worship God in spirit and truth'

Jesus declared, 'Believe me, woman, a time is coming when you will worship the Father neither on this mountain nor in Jerusalem. You Samaritans worship what you do not know; we worship what we do know, for salvation is from the Jews. Yet a time is coming and has now come when the true worshippers will worship the Father in spirit and truth, for they are the kind of worshippers the Father seeks. God is spirit, and his worshippers must worship in spirit and in truth.'

The woman said, 'I know that Messiah' (called Christ) 'is coming. When he comes, he will explain everything to us.'

Then Jesus declared, 'I who speak to you am he.'

Just then his disciples returned and were surprised to find him talking with a woman. But no-one asked, 'What do you want?' or 'Why are you talking with her?'

Then, leaving her water jar, the woman went back to the town and said to the people, 'Come, see a man who told me everything I ever did. Could this be the Christ?' They came out of the town and made their way towards him . . .

'This man really is the Saviour of the world'

Many of the Samaritans from that town believed in him because of the woman's testimony, 'He told me everything I ever did.' So when the Samaritans came to him, they urged him to stay with them, and he stayed two days. And because of his words many more became believers.

They said to the woman, 'We no longer believe just because of what you said; now we have heard for ourselves, and we know that this man really is the Saviour of the world.'   JOHN 4:7–30; 39–42

6. A woman caught in adultery

But Jesus went to the Mount of Olives. At dawn he appeared

again in the temple courts, where all the people gathered round him, and he sat down to teach them. The teachers of the law and the Pharisees brought in a woman caught in adultery. They made her stand before the group and said to Jesus, 'Teacher, this woman was caught in the act of adultery. In the Law Moses commanded us to stone such women. Now what do you say?' They were using this question as a trap, in order to have a basis for accusing him.

But Jesus bent down and started to write on the ground with his finger. When they kept on questioning him, he straightened up and said to them, 'Let anyone of you who is without sin be the first to throw a stone at her.' Again he stooped down and wrote on the ground.

'Go now and leave your life of sin'

At this, those who heard began to go away one at a time, the older ones first, until only Jesus was left, with the woman still standing there. Jesus straightened up and asked her, 'Woman, where are they? Has no-one condemned you?'

'No-one, sir,' she said.

'Then neither do I condemn you,' Jesus declared. 'Go now and leave your life of sin.'   JOHN 8:1–11

7. Some Greeks

Now there were some Greeks among those who went up to worship at the Feast. They came to Philip, who was from Bethsaida in Galilee, with a request. 'Sir,' they said, 'we would like to see Jesus.' Philip went to tell Andrew; Andrew and Philip in turn told Jesus.

'Whoever serves me must follow me'

Jesus replied, 'The hour has come for the Son of Man to be glorified. I tell you the truth, unless a grain of wheat falls to the ground and dies, it remains only a single seed. But if it dies, it produces many seeds. Those who love their lives will lose them, while those who hate their lives in this world will keep them for eternal life. Whoever serves me must follow me; and where I am, my servant also will be. My Father will honour the one who serves me.'   JOHN 12:20–26

8. Children

People were bringing little children to Jesus to have him touch them, but the disciples rebuked them. When Jesus saw this, he was indignant. He said to them, 'Let the little children come to me, and do not hinder them, for the kingdom of God belongs to such as these. I tell you the truth, anyone who will not receive the kingdom of God like a little child will never enter it.' And he took the children in his arms, put his hands on them and blessed them.   MARK 10:13–16

F. Family, home town and friends

1. Jesus' mother and brothers

While Jesus was still talking to the crowd, his mother and brothers stood outside, wanting to speak to him. Someone told him, 'Your mother and brothers are standing outside, wanting to speak to you.'

He replied, 'Who is my mother, and who are my brothers?' Pointing to his disciples, he said, 'Here are my mother and my brothers. For whoever does the will of my Father in heaven is my brother and sister and mother.'   MATTHEW 12:46–50

2. The synagogue in Nazareth

He went to Nazareth, where he had been brought up, and on

the Sabbath day he went into the synagogue, as was his custom. And he stood up to read. The scroll of the prophet Isaiah was handed to him. Unrolling it, he found the place where it is written:

'The Spirit of the Lord is on me,
    because he has anointed me
    to preach good news to the poor.
He has sent me to proclaim freedom for the prisoners
    and recovery of sight for the blind,
to release the oppressed,
    to proclaim the year of the Lord's favour.'

'Today this scripture is fulfilled in your hearing'

Then he rolled up the scroll, gave it back to the attendant and sat down. The eyes of everyone in the synagogue were fastened on him, and he began by saying to them, 'Today this scripture is fulfilled in your hearing.'

All spoke well of him and were amazed at the gracious words that came from his lips. 'Isn't this Joseph's son?' they asked.

Jesus said to them, 'Surely you will quote this proverb to me: "Physician, heal yourself! Do here in your home town what we have heard that you did in Capernaum."'

'I tell you the truth,' he continued, 'prophets are not accepted in their home towns. I assure you that there were many widows in Israel in Elijah's time, when the sky was shut for three and a half years and there was a severe famine throughout the land. Yet Elijah was not sent to any of them, but to a widow in Zarephath in the region of Sidon. And there were many in Israel with leprosy in the time of Elisha the prophet, yet not one of them was cleansed – only Naaman the Syrian.'

They drove Jesus out of the town

All the people in the synagogue were furious when they heard this. They got up, drove him out of the town, and took him to the brow of the hill on which the town was built, in order to throw him down the cliff. But he walked right through the crowd and went on his way.   LUKE 4:16–30

3. A mother's request

Then the mother of Zebedee's sons came to Jesus with her sons and, kneeling down, asked a favour of him.

'What is it you want?' he asked.

She said, 'Grant that one of these two sons of mine may sit at your right and the other at your left in your kingdom.'

'You don't know what you are asking,' Jesus said to them, 'Can you drink the cup I am going to drink?'

'We can,' they answered.

Jesus said to them, 'You will indeed drink from my cup, but to sit at my right or left is not for me to grant. These places belong to those for whom they have been prepared by my Father.'

The ten were indignant

When the ten heard about this, they were indignant with the two brothers. Jesus called them together and said, 'You know that the rulers of the Gentiles lord it over them, and their high officials exercise authority over them. Not so with you. Instead, whoever wants to become great among you must be your servant, and whoever wants to be first must be your slave – just as the Son of Man did not come to be served, but to serve, and to give his life as a ransom for many.'   MATTHEW 20:20–28

4. Martha

'Martha, Martha,' the Lord answered, 'you are worried and upset about many things, but only one thing is needed. Mary has chosen what is better, and it will not be taken away from her.'   LUKE 10:41–42

❧ THE TEACHING OF JESUS ❧

A. The Sermon on the Mount

1. The Beatitudes

Now when he saw the crowds, he went up on a mountainside and sat down. His disciples came to him, and he began to teach them, saying:
'Blessed are the poor in spirit,
  for theirs is the kingdom of heaven.
Blessed are those who mourn,
  for they will be comforted.
Blessed are the meek,
  for they will inherit the earth.
Blessed are those who hunger and thirst for righteousness,
  for they will be filled.
Blessed are the merciful,
  for they will be shown mercy.
Blessed are the pure in heart,
  for they will see God.
Blessed are the peacemakers,
  for they will be called children of God.
Blessed are those who are persecuted because of
    righteousness,
  for theirs is the kingdom of heaven.
'Blessed are you when people insult you, persecute you and falsely say all kinds of evil against you because of me. Rejoice and be glad, because great is your reward in heaven, for in the same way they persecuted the prophets who were before you.' MATTHEW 5:1–12

'Woe to you who are rich,
  for you have already received your comfort.
Woe to you who are well fed now,
  for you will go hungry.

65

Woe to you who laugh now,
    for you will mourn and weep.
Woe to you when everyone speaks well of you,
    for that is how their ancestors treated the false prophets.'
LUKE 6:24–26

2. Salt and light

'You are the salt of the earth. But if the salt loses its saltiness,
how can it be made salty again? It is no longer good for anything, except to be thrown out and trampled under foot.

'You are the light of the world. A city on a hill cannot be hidden. Neither do people light a lamp and put it under a bowl.
Instead they put it on its stand, and it gives light to everyone
in the house. In the same way, let your light shine before
others, that they may see your good deeds and praise your
Father in heaven.'   MATTHEW 5:13–16

3. Teaching about the law

'Do not think that I have come to abolish the Law or the
Prophets; I have not come to abolish them but to fulfil them.
I tell you the truth, until heaven and earth disappear, not the
smallest letter, not the least stroke of a pen, will by any means
disappear from the Law until everything is accomplished. Anyone who breaks one of the least of these commandments and
teaches others to do the same will be called least in the kingdom of heaven, but whoever practises and teaches these commands will be called great in the kingdom of heaven. For I tell
you that unless your righteousness surpasses that of the
Pharisees and the teachers of the law, you will certainly not
enter the kingdom of heaven.   MATTHEW 5:17–20

4. Teaching about anger

'You have heard that it was said to the people long ago, "Do not murder, and anyone who murders will be subject to judgment." But I tell you that anyone who is angry with a brother or sister will be subject to judgment. Again, anyone who says to a brother or sister, "Raca," is answerable to the Sanhedrin. But anyone who says "You fool!" will be in danger of the fire of hell.

'Therefore, if you are offering your gift at the altar and there remember that your brother or sister has something against you, leave your gift there in front of the altar. First go and be reconciled to them; then come and offer your gift.'   MATTHEW 5:21–24

5. Settle disputes

'Settle matters quickly with your adversary who is taking you to court. Do it while you are still together on the way, or your adversary may hand you over to the judge, and the judge may hand you over to the officer, and you may be thrown in prison. I tell you the truth, you will not get out until you have paid the last penny.'   MATTHEW 5:25–26

6. Teaching about adultery

'You have heard that it was said, "Do not commit adultery." But I tell you that anyone who looks at a woman lustfully has already committed adultery with her in his heart. If your right eye causes you to sin, gouge it out and throw it away. It is better for you to lose one part of your body than for your whole body to be thrown into hell. And if your right hand causes you to sin, cut it off and throw it away. It is better for you to lose one part of your body than for your whole body to go into hell.'   MATTHEW 5:27–30

7. Teaching about divorce

'It has been said, "Anyone who divorces his wife must give her a certificate of divorce." But I tell you that anyone who divorces his wife, except for marital unfaithfulness, causes her to become an adulteress, and anyone who marries the divorced woman commits adultery.'   MATTHEW 5:31-32

8. Teaching about oaths

'Again, you have heard that it was said to the people long ago, "Do not break your oath, but keep the oaths you have made to the Lord." But I tell you, Do not swear at all: either by heaven, for it is God's throne; or by the earth, for it is his footstool; or by Jerusalem, for it is the city of the Great King. And do not swear by your head, for you cannot make even one hair white or black. Simply let your "Yes" be "Yes", and your "No", "No"; anything beyond this comes from the evil one.'   MATTHEW 5:33-37

9. Teaching about revenge

'You have heard that it was said, "Eye for eye, and tooth for tooth." But I tell you, Do not resist an evil person. If someone strikes you on the right cheek, turn the other cheek also. And if someone wants to sue you and take your tunic, hand over your cloak as well. If someone forces you to go one mile, go two miles. Give to the one who asks you, and do not turn away from the one who wants to borrow from you.'   MATTHEW 5:38-42

10. Love your enemies

'You have heard that it was said, "Love your neighbour and hate your enemy." But I tell you: Love your enemies and pray for those who persecute you, that you may be children of your

Father in heaven. He causes his sun to rise on the evil and the good, and sends rain on the righteous and the unrighteous. If you love those who love you, what reward will you get? Are not even the tax collectors doing that? And if you greet only your own people, what are you doing more than others? Do not even pagans do that? Be perfect, therefore, as your heavenly Father is perfect.'   MATTHEW 5:43–48

'Be merciful, just as your Father is merciful.'   LUKE 6:36

11. Giving to the needy

'Be careful not to do your "acts of righteousness" before others, to be seen by them. If you do, you will have no reward from your Father in heaven.

'So when you give to the needy, do not announce it with trumpets, as the hypocrites do in the synagogues and on the streets, to be honoured by others. I tell you the truth, they have received their reward in full. But when you give to the needy, do not let your left hand know what your right hand is doing, so that your giving may be in secret. Then your Father, who sees what is done in secret, will reward you.'   MATTHEW 6:1–4

12. Teaching about fasting

'When you fast, do not look sombre as the hypocrites do, for they disfigure their faces to show men they are fasting. I tell you the truth, they have received their reward in full. But when you fast, put oil on your head and wash your face, so that it will not be obvious to others that you are fasting , but only to your Father, who is unseen; and your Father, who sees what is done in secret, will reward you.'   MATTHEW 6:16–18

13. Treasures in heaven

'Do not store up for yourselves treasures on earth, where moth and rust destroy, and where thieves break in and steal. But store up for yourselves treasures in heaven, where moth and rust do not destroy, and where thieves do not break in and steal. For where your treasure is, there your heart will be also.' MATTHEW 6:19–21

14. 'The eye is the lamp of the body'

'The eye is the lamp of the body. If your eyes are good, your whole body will be full of light. But if your eyes are bad, your whole body will be full of darkness. If then the light within you is darkness, how great is that darkness!' MATTHEW 6:22–23

15. God and Money

'No-one can be a slave to two masters. Either you will hate the one and love the other or you will be devoted to the one and despise the other. You cannot be a slave to both God and Money.' MATTHEW 6:24

16. Do not worry

'Therefore I tell you, do not worry about your life, what you will eat or drink; or about your body, what you will wear. Is not life more important than food, and the body more important than clothes? Look at the birds of the air; they do not sow or reap or store away in barns, and yet your heavenly Father feeds them. Are you not much more valuable than they? Who of you by worrying can add a single hour to your life?

'And why do you worry about clothes? See how the lilies of the field grow. They do not labour or spin. Yet I tell you that not even Solomon in all his splendour was dressed like one of these. If that is how God clothes the grass of the field, which is here today and tomorrow is thrown into the fire, will he not much more clothe you, O you of little faith? So do not worry, saying, "What shall we eat?" or "What shall we drink?" or "What shall we wear?" For the pagans run after all these things, and your heavenly Father knows that you need them. But seek first his kingdom and his righteousness, and all these things will be given to you as well. Therefore do not worry about tomorrow, for tomorrow will worry about itself. Each day has enough trouble of its own.'   MATTHEW 6:25–34

17. Don't judge others

'Do not judge, or you too will be judged. For in the same way as you judge others, you will be judged, and with the measure you use, it will be measured to you.

'Why do you look at the speck of sawdust in someone else's eye and pay no attention to the plank in your own eye? How can you say, "Let me take the speck out of your eye," when all the time there is a plank in your own eye? You hypocrite, first take the plank out of your own eye, and then you will see clearly to remove the speck from the other person's eye.'   MATTHEW 7:1–5

18. Don't profane sacred things

'Do not give dogs what is sacred; do not throw your pearls to pigs. If you do, they may trample them under their feet, and then turn and tear you to pieces.'   MATTHEW 7:6

B. Jesus teaches his disciples

1. Jesus' death and suffering

From that time on Jesus began to explain to his disciples that he must go to Jerusalem and suffer many things at the hands of the elders, chief priests and teachers of the law, and that he must be killed and on the third day be raised to life.

Peter took him aside and began to rebuke him. 'Never, Lord!' he said. 'This shall never happen to you!'

Jesus turned and said to Peter, 'Get behind me, Satan! You are a stumbling-block to me; you do not have in mind the concerns of God, but human concerns.'   MATTHEW 16:21–23

2. Jesus speaks about his death and resurrection

'The Son of Man is going to be betrayed into human hands. People will kill him, and on the third day he will be raised to life.'   MATTHEW 17:22–23

3. Leading others astray

'If any of you causes one of these little ones who believe in me to sin, it would be better for you to have a large millstone hung around your neck and to be drowned in the depths of the sea.

'Woe to the world because of the things that cause people to sin! Such things must come, but woe to the person through whom they come!'   MATTHEW 18:6–7

4. A brother or sister who sins against you

'If your brother or sister sins against you, go and show them their fault, just between the two of you. If they listen to you,

you have won them over. But if they will not listen, take one or two others along, so that "every matter may be established by the testimony of two or three witnesses". If they refuse to listen to them, tell it to the church; and if they refuse to listen even to the church, treat them as you would a pagan or a tax collector.

'I tell you the truth, whatever you bind on earth will be bound in heaven, and whatever you loose on earth will be loosed in heaven.'   MATTHEW 18:15–18

5. Rich people and God's kingdom

Jesus looked around and said to his disciples, 'How hard it is for the rich to enter the kingdom of God!'

The disciples were amazed at his words. But Jesus said again, 'Children, how hard it is to enter the kingdom of God! It is easier for a camel to go through the eye of a needle than for a rich man to enter the kingdom of God.'   MARK 10:23–25

6. 'Whoever is not against us is for us'

'Teacher,' said John, 'we saw someone driving out demons in your name and we told him to stop, because he was not one of us.'

'Do not stop him,' Jesus said. 'No-one who does a miracle in my name can in the next moment say anything bad about me, for whoever is not against us is for us.'   MARK 9:38–40

7. 'Two very small copper coins'

Jesus sat down opposite the place where the offerings were put and watched the crowd putting their money into the temple treasury. Many rich people threw in large amounts. But a poor widow came and put in two very small copper coins, worth only a fraction of a penny.

Calling his disciples to him, Jesus said, 'I tell you the truth, this poor widow has put more into the treasury than all the others. They all gave out of their wealth; but she, out of her poverty, put in everything – all she had to live on.'   MARK 12:41–44

8. Instructions for the twelve disciples

'Preach . . . heal'
These twelve Jesus sent out with the following instructions: 'Do not go among the Gentiles or enter any town of the Samaritans. Go rather to the lost sheep of Israel.

'As you go, preach this message: "The kingdom of heaven is near."

'Heal the sick, raise the dead, cleanse those who have leprosy, drive out demons. Freely you have received, freely give.

'Do not take along any gold or silver or copper in your belts; take no bag for the journey, or extra tunic, or sandals or a staff; for workers are worth their keep.

'Whatever town or village you enter, search for some worthy person there and stay at that house until you leave. As you enter the home, give it your greeting. If the home is deserving, let your peace rest on it; if it is not, let your peace return to you. If anyone will not welcome you or listen to your words, shake the dust off your feet when you leave that home or town. I tell you the truth, it will be more bearable for Sodom and Gomorrah on the day of judgment than for that town.'   MATTHEW 10:5–15

9. 'Be shrewd as snakes and innocent as doves'

'I am sending you out like sheep among wolves. Therefore be as shrewd as snakes and as innocent as doves. Be on your guard against other people; they will hand you over to the local councils and flog you in their synagogues. On my account you will be brought before governors and kings as witnesses to them and to the Gentiles. But when they arrest you, do not worry about what to say or how to say it. At that time you will be given what to say, for it will not be you speaking, but the Spirit of your Father speaking through you.' MATTHEW 10:16-20

10. Expect persecution

'Brother will betray brother to death, and a father his child; children will rebel against their parents and have them put to death. Everyone will hate you because of me, but those who stand firm to the end will be saved. When you are persecuted in one place, flee to another. I tell you the truth, you will not finish going through the cities of Israel before the Son of Man comes.

'Students are not above their teachers, nor servants above their masters. It is enough for students to be like their teachers, and servants like their masters. If the head of the house has been called Beelzebub, how much more the members of the household!' MATTHEW 10:21-25

11. Whom to fear

'So do not be afraid of them. There is nothing concealed that will not be disclosed, or hidden that will not be made known. What I tell you in the dark, speak in the daylight; what is whispered in your ear, proclaim from the roofs. Do not be afraid of those who kill the body but cannot kill the soul. Rather, be afraid of the One who can destroy both soul and body in hell. Are not two sparrows sold for a penny? Yet not one of them will fall to the ground apart from the will of your Father. And even the very hairs of your head are all numbered. So don't be afraid; you are worth more than many sparrows.' MATTHEW 10:26-31

12. Acknowledging and disowning Jesus

'Those who acknowledge me before others, I will also

acknowledge before my Father in heaven. But those who disown me before others, I will disown before my Father in heaven.' MATTHEW 10:32–33

13. Not peace, but division

'Do not suppose that I have come to bring peace to the earth. I did not come to bring peace, but a sword.' MATTHEW 10:37

'I have come to bring fire on the earth, and how I wish it were already kindled! But I have a baptism to undergo, and how distressed I am until it is completed! Do you think I came to bring peace on earth? No, I tell you, but division. From now on there will be five in one family divided against each other, three against two and two against three. They will be divided, father against son and son against father, mother against daughter and daughter against mother, mother-in-law against daughter-in-law and daughter-in-law against mother-in-law.' LUKE 12:49–53

14. Rewards

'Anyone who loves father or mother more than me is not worthy of me; anyone who loves son or daughter more than me is not worthy of me. Those who do not take up their cross and follow me are not worthy of me. Those who find their lives will lose them, and those who lose their lives for my sake will find them.' MATTHEW 10:37–39

15. 'Rebuke a brother or sister who sins'

'Rebuke a brother or sister who sins, and if they repent, forgive them. If anyone sins against you seven times in a day, and seven times comes back to you and says, "I repent," you must forgive them.' LUKE 17:3–4

16. 'Increase our faith!'

The apostles said to the Lord, 'Increase our faith!'

He replied, 'If you have faith as small as a mustard seed, you can say to this mulberry tree, "Be uprooted and planted in the sea," and it will obey you.' LUKE 17:5–6

17. Humble service

'Suppose one of you had a servant ploughing or looking after the sheep. Would he say to the servant when he comes in from the field, "Come along now and sit down to eat"? Would he not rather say, "Prepare my supper, get yourself ready and wait on me while I eat and drink; after that you may eat and drink"? Would he thank the servant because he did what he was told to do? So you also, when you have done everything you were told to do, should say, "We are unworthy servants; we have only done our duty."' LUKE 17:7–10

18. 'Who is the greatest?'

Also a dispute arose among them as to which of them was considered to be greatest. Jesus said to them, 'The kings of the Gentiles lord it over them; and those who exercise authority over them call themselves Benefactors. But you are not to be like that. Instead, the greatest among you should be like the youngest, and the one who rules like the one who serves.'

'I am among you as one who serves'
'For who is greater, the one who is at the table or the one who serves? Is it not the one who is at the table? But I am among you as one who serves.' LUKE 22:24–30

19. A time of crisis

Then Jesus asked them, 'When I sent you without purse, bag or sandals, did you lack anything?'

'Nothing,' they answered.

He said to them, 'But now if you have a purse, take it, and also a bag; and if you don't have a sword, sell your cloak and buy one. It is written: "And he was numbered with the transgressors"; and I tell you that this must be fulfilled in me. Yes, what is written about me is reaching its fulfilment.'

The disciples said, 'See, Lord, here are two swords.'

'That is enough,' he replied.   LUKE 22:35–38

20. Jesus promises the Holy Spirit

'And I will ask the Father, and he will give you another Counsellor to be with you for ever – the Spirit of truth. The world cannot accept him, because it neither sees him nor knows him. But you know him, for he lives with you and will be in you. I will not leave you as orphans; I will come to you. Before long, the world will not see me any more, but you will see me. Because I live, you also will live. On that day you will realise that I am in my Father, and you are in me, and I am in you. Those who have my commands and obey them are the ones who love me. Those who love me will be loved by my Father, and I too will love them and show myself to them.'
JOHN 14:16–21

21. The Holy Spirit will teach you

Then Judas (not Judas Iscariot) said, 'But, Lord, why do you intend to show yourself to us and not to the world?'

Jesus replied, 'Those who love me will obey my teaching. My Father will love them, and we will come to them and make our home with them. Anyone who does not love me will not obey my teaching. These words you hear are not my own; they belong to the Father who sent me.'

'The Counsellor will teach you all things'

'All this I have spoken while still with you. But the Counsellor, the Holy Spirit, whom the Father will send in my name, will teach you all things and will remind you of everything I have said to you. Peace I leave with you; my peace I give you. I do not give to you as the world gives. Do not let your hearts be troubled and do not be afraid.

'You heard me say, "I am going away and I am coming back to you." If you loved me, you would be glad that I am going to the Father, for the Father is greater than I. I have told you now before it happens, so that when it does happen you will believe. I will not speak with you much longer, for the prince of this world is coming. He has no hold on me.'   JOHN 14:22–30

22. 'Love each other as I have loved you'

'I have told you this so that my joy may be in you and that your joy may be complete. My command is this: Love each other as I have loved you. Greater love has no-one than this, to lay down one's life for one's friends. You are my friends if you do what I command. I no longer call you servants, because servants do not know their master's business. Instead, I have called you friends, for everything that I learned from my Father I have made known to you. You did not choose me, but I chose you and appointed you to go and bear fruit – fruit that will last. Then the Father will give you whatever you ask in my name. This is my command: Love each other.'   JOHN 15:11–17

23. 'If they persecuted me, they will persecute you also'

'If the world hates you, keep in mind that it hated me first. If you belonged to the world, it would love you as its own. As it is, you do not belong to the world, but I have chosen you out of the world. That is why the world hates you. Remember the words I spoke to you: "Servants are not greater than their masters." If they persecuted me, they will persecute you also. If they obeyed my teaching, they will obey yours also. They will treat you this way because of my name, for they do not know the One who sent me. If I had not come and spoken to them, they would not be guilty of sin. Now, however, they have no excuse for their sin. Those who hate me hate my Father as well. If I had not done among them what no-one else did, they would not be guilty of sin. But now they have seen these miracles, and yet they have hated both me and my Father. But this is to fulfil what is written in their Law: "They hated me without reason."   JOHN 15:18–25

24. The Holy Spirit will speak about Jesus

'When the Counsellor comes, whom I will send to you from the Father, the Spirit of truth who goes out from the Father, he will testify about me. And you also must testify, for you have been with me from the beginning.'   JOHN 15:26–27

25. Christian martyrs

'All this I have told you so that you will not go astray. They will put you out of the synagogue; in fact, a time is coming when those who kill you will think they are offering a service to God. They will do such things because they have not known the Father or me. I have told you this, so that when the time comes you will remember that I warned you. I did not tell you this at first because I was with you.'   JOHN 16:1–4

26. 'The Spirit will give me glory'

'Now I am going to him who sent me, yet none of you asks me,

"Where are you going?" Because I have said these things, you are filled with grief. But I tell you the truth: It is for your good that I am going away. Unless I go away, the Counsellor will not come to you; but if I go, I will send him to you. When he comes, he will convict the world of guilt in regard to sin and righteousness and judgment: in regard to sin, because people do not believe in me; in regard to righteousness, because I am going to the Father, where you can see me no longer; and in regard to judgment, because the prince of this world now stands condemned.'

'The Spirit will guide you into all truth'

'I have much more to say to you, more than you can now bear. But when he, the Spirit of truth, comes, he will guide you into all truth. He will not speak on his own; he will speak only what he hears, and he will tell you what is yet to come. He will bring glory to me by taking from what is mine and making it known to you. All that belongs to the Father is mine. That is why I said the Spirit will take from what is mine and make it known to you.'   JOHN 16:5–15

27. Peace in a troubled world

'You believe at last!' Jesus answered. 'But a time is coming, and has come, when you will be scattered, each to his own home. You will leave me all alone. Yet I am not alone, for my Father is with me.

'I have told you these things, so that in me you may have peace. In this world you will have trouble. But take heart! I have overcome the world.'   JOHN 16:31–33

28. Jesus gives marching orders

Then the eleven disciples went to Galilee, to the mountain where Jesus had told them to go. When they saw him, they worshipped him; but some doubted. Then Jesus came to them and said, 'All authority in heaven and on earth has been given to me. Therefore go and make disciples of all nations, baptising them in the name of the Father and of the Son and of the Holy Spirit, and teaching them to obey everything I have commanded you. And surely I am with you always, to the very end of the age.' MATTHEW 28:16–20

C. Jesus teaches the crowds

1. Turn from your sins or die

'Unless you repent, you too will all perish'
Now there were some present at that time who told Jesus about the Galileans whose blood Pilate had mixed with their sacrifices. Jesus answered, 'Do you think that these Galileans were worse sinners than all the other Galileans because they suffered in this way? I tell you, no! But unless you repent, you too will all perish. Or those eighteen who died when the tower in Siloam fell on them – do you think they were more guilty than all the others living in Jerusalem? I tell you, no! But unless you repent, you too will all perish.'

'A man had a fig-tree . . .'
Then he told this parable: 'A man had a fig-tree, planted in his vineyard, and he went to look for fruit on it, but did not find any. So he said to the man who took care of the vineyard, "For three years now I've been coming to look for fruit on this fig-tree and haven't found any. Cut it down! Why should it use up the soil?"

'"Sir," the man replied, "leave it alone for one more year, and I'll dig round it and fertilise it. If it bears fruit next year, fine! If not, then cut it down."' LUKE 13:6–9

2. 'Work for food that endures to eternal life'

'I tell you the truth, you are looking for me, not because you
saw miraculous signs but because you ate the loaves and had
your fill. Do not work for food that spoils, but for food that
endures to eternal life, which the Son of Man will give you. On
him God the Father has placed his seal of approval.' JOHN 6:26–27

3. 'Who are you?'

'My other witness is the Father, who sent me'

When Jesus spoke again to the people, he said, 'I am the light of
the world. Whoever follows me will never walk in darkness, but
will have the light of life.'

The Pharisees challenged him, 'Here you are, appearing as
your own witness; your testimony is not valid.'

Jesus answered, 'Even if I testify on my own behalf, my testimony is valid, for I know where I came from and where I am
going. But you have no idea where I come from or where I am
going. You judge by human standards; I pass judgment on no-
one. But if I do judge, my decisions are right, because I am not
alone. I stand with the Father who sent me. In your own Law it
is written that the testimony of two witnesses is valid. I am one
who testifies for myself; my other witness is the Father, who
who sent me.'

Then they asked him, 'Where is your father?'

'You do not know me or my Father,' Jesus replied. 'If you
knew me, you would know my Father also.' He spoke these
words while teaching in the temple area near the place where
the offerings were put. Yet no-one seized him, because his time
had not yet come.

Once more Jesus said to them, 'I am going away, and you
will look for me, and you will die in your sin. Where I go, you
cannot come.'

This made the Jews ask, 'Will he kill himself? Is that why he
says, "Where I go you cannot come"?'

'You are of this world; I am not of this world'

But he continued, 'You are from below; I am from above. You are of this world; I am not of this world. I told you that you would die in your sins; if you do not believe that I am the one I claim to be, you will indeed die in your sins.'

'Who are you?' they asked.

'Just what I have been claiming all along,' Jesus replied. 'I have much to say in judgment of you. But he who sent me is reliable, and what I have heard from him I tell the world.'

They did not understand that he was telling them about his Father. So Jesus said, 'When you have lifted up the Son of Man, then you will know that I am the one I claim to be and that I do nothing on my own but speak just what the Father has taught me. The one who sent me is with me; he has not left me alone, for I always do what pleases him.' Even as he spoke, many put their faith in him.   JOHN 8:12–30

4. 'I have come into the world as a light'

Then Jesus cried out, 'Those who believe in me do not believe in me only, but in the one who sent me. When they look at me, they see the one who sent me. I have come into the world as a light, so that no-one who believes in me should stay in darkness.

'As for those who hear my words but do not keep them, I do not judge them. For I did not come to judge the world, but to save it. There is a judge for those who reject me and do not accept my words; that very word which I spoke will condemn them at the last day. For I did not speak of my own accord, but the Father who sent me commanded me what to say and how to say it. I know that his command leads to eternal life. So whatever I say is just what the Father has told me to say.'   JOHN 12:44–50

D. Parables about the kingdom of heaven

1. The growing seed

He also said, 'This is what the kingdom of God is like. A man scatters seed on the ground. Night and day, whether he sleeps or gets up, the seed sprouts and grows, though he does not know how. All by itself the soil produces corn – first the stalk, then the ear, then the full grain in the ear. As soon as the grain is ripe, he puts the sickle to it, because the harvest has come.' MARK 4:26–29

2. The weeds

Jesus told them another parable: 'The kingdom of heaven is like a man who sowed good seed in his field. But while everyone was sleeping, his enemy came and sowed weeds among the wheat, and went away. When the wheat sprouted and formed ears, then the weeds also appeared.

'The owner's servants came to him and said, "Sir, didn't you sow good seed in your field? Where then did the weeds come from?"

'"An enemy did this," he replied.

'The servants asked him, "Do you want us to go and pull them up?"

'"No," he answered, "because while you are pulling the weeds, you may root up the wheat with them. Let both grow together until the harvest. At that time I will tell the harvesters: First collect the weeds and tie them in bundles to be burned, then gather the wheat and bring it into my barn."'

'The weeds are the sons of the evil one'
Then he left the crowd and went into the house. His disciples came to him and said, 'Explain to us the parable of the weeds in the field.'

All the parables of Jesus

	MATTHEW	MARK	LUKE
Lamp under bowl	5:14–15	4:21–22	8:16; 11:33
Houses on rock and sand	7:24–27		6:47–49
New cloth on old coat	9:16	2:21	5:36
New wine in old wineskins	9:17	2:22	5:37–38
The sower	13:3–8; 18–23	4:3–8; 14–20	8:4–8; 11–15
The weeds	13:24–30; 36–43		
The mustard seed	13:31–32	4:30–32	13:18–19
Yeast	13:33		13:20–21
Hidden treasure	13:44		
Fine pearls	13:45–46		
The fisherman's net	13:47–50		
The homeowner	13:51–52		
The lost sheep	18:12–14		15:4–7
The unforgiving servant	18:23–34		
Workers in the vineyard	20:1–16		
The two sons	21:28–32		
The tenants in the vineyard	21:33–46	12:1–9	20:9–16
The wedding banquet	22:2–14		
The lesson of the fig-tree	24:32–33	13:28–29	21:29–32
The faithful servant	24:45–51		12:42–48
The ten virgins	25:1–13		
Using money	25:14–30		19:11–27
The sheep and the goats	25:31–46		

All the parables of Jesus

	MATTHEW	MARK	LUKE
The growing seed		4:26–29	
The money-lender and two debtors			7:41–43
'Who is my neighbour?'			10:25–37
The friend at midnight			11:5–8
The rich fool			12:13–21
Watchful servants			12:35–40
The fig-tree without figs			13:6–9
Humility and hospitality			14:7–11
The great banquet			14:15–24
The cost of being a disciple			14:28–33
The lost coin			15:8–10
The runaway son			15:11–32
The shrewd manager			16:1–12
The rich man and Lazarus			16:19–31
The master and his servant			17:7–10
The widow and the judge			18:2–5
The Pharisee and the tax collector			18:9–14

He answered, 'The one who sowed the good seed is the Son of Man. The field is the world, and the good seed stands for the people of the kingdom. The weeds are the people of the evil one, and the enemy who sows them is the devil. The harvest is the end of the age, and the harvesters are angels.

'As the weeds are pulled up and burned in the fire, so it will be at the end of the age. The Son of Man will send out his angels, and they will weed out of his kingdom everything that causes sin and all who do evil. They will throw them into the fiery furnace, where there will be weeping and gnashing of teeth. Then the righteous will shine like the sun in the kingdom of their Father. Those who have ears, let them hear.

MATTHEW 13:24–30; 36–43

3. The mustard seed

He told them another parable: 'The kingdom of heaven is like a mustard seed which a man took and planted in his field. Though it is the smallest of all your seeds, yet when it grows, it is the largest of garden plants and becomes a tree, so that the birds of the air come and perch in its branches.'   MATTHEW 13:31–32

4. Yeast

He told them still another parable, 'The kingdom of heaven is like yeast that a woman took and mixed into a large amount of flour until it worked all through the dough.'   MATTHEW 13:33

5. Hidden treasure

'The kingdom of heaven is like treasure hidden in a field. When a man found it, he hid it again, and then in his joy went and sold all he had and bought that field.'   MATTHEW 13:44

6. Fine pearls

'Again, the kingdom of heaven is like a merchant looking for fine pearls. When he found one of great value, he went away and sold everything he had and bought it.'   MATTHEW 13:45–46

7. The fisherman's net

'Once again, the kingdom of heaven is like a net that was let down into the lake and caught all kinds of fish. When it was full, the fishermen pulled it up on the shore. Then they sat down and collected the good fish in baskets, but threw the bad away. This is how it will be at the end of the age. The angels will come and separate the wicked from the righteous and throw them into the fiery furnace, where there will be weeping and gnashing of teeth.'   MATTHEW 13:47–50

8. The homeowner

'Have you understood all these things?' Jesus asked.

'Yes,' they replied.

He said to them, 'Therefore every teacher of the law who has been instructed about the kingdom of heaven is like the owner of a house who brings out of the storeroom new treasures as well as old.'   MATTHEW 13:51–52

9. Workers in the vineyard

'For the kingdom of heaven is like a landowner who went out early in the morning to hire workers for his vineyard. He agreed to pay them a denarius for the day and sent them into his vineyard.

'About the third hour he went out and saw others standing in the market-place doing nothing. He told them, "You also go

and work in my vineyard, and I will pay you whatever is right."
So they went.

'He went out again about the sixth hour and the ninth hour
and did the same thing. About the eleventh hour he went out
and found still others standing around. He asked them, "Why
have you been standing here all day long doing nothing?"

'"Because no-one has hired us," they answered.

'He said to them, "You also go and work in my vineyard."

'When evening came, the owner of the vineyard said to his
manager, "Call the workers and pay them their wages, beginning with the last ones hired and going on to the first."

'The last will be first, and the first will be last'
'The workers who were hired about the eleventh hour came
and each received a denarius. So when those came who were
hired first, they expected to receive more. But each one of
them also received a denarius. When they received it, they
began to grumble against the landowner. "These people who
were hired last worked only one hour," they said, "and you
have made them equal to us who have borne the burden of the
work and the heat of the day."

'But he answered one of them, "Friend, I am not being unfair
to you. Didn't you agree to work for a denarius? Take your pay
and go. I want to give the one who was hired last the same as I
gave you. Don't I have the right to do what I want with my own
money? Or are you envious because I am generous?"

'So the last will be first, and the first will be last.'   MATTHEW
20:1–16

10. The two sons

'What do you think? There was a man who had two sons. He went
to the first and said, "Son, go and work today in the vineyard."

'"I will not," he answered, but later he changed his mind and
went.

'Then the father went to the other son and said the same

thing. He answered, "I will, sir," but he did not go.

'Which of the two did what his father wanted?'

'The first,' they answered.

Jesus said to them, 'I tell you the truth, the tax collectors and the prostitutes are entering the kingdom of God ahead of you. For John came to you to show you the way of righteousness, and you did not believe him, but the tax collectors and the prostitutes did. And even after you saw this, you did not repent and believe him.' MATTHEW 21:28-32

11. The wedding banquet

They refused to come

'The kingdom of heaven is like a king who prepared a wedding banquet for his son. He sent his servants to those who had been invited to the banquet to tell them to come, but they refused to come.

'Then he sent some more servants and said, "Tell those who have been invited that I have prepared my dinner: My oxen and fattened cattle have been slaughtered, and everything is ready. Come to the wedding banquet."

'But they paid no attention and went off – one to his field, another to his business. The rest seized his servants, ill-treated them and killed them. The king was enraged. He sent his army and destroyed those murderers and burned their city.

'Then he said to his servants, "The wedding banquet is ready, but those I invited did not deserve to come. Go to the street corners and invite to the banquet anyone you find." So the servants went out into the streets and gathered all the people they could find, both good and bad, and the wedding hall was filled with guests.'

'Many are invited, but few are chosen'

'But when the king came in to see the guests, he noticed a man there who was not wearing wedding clothes. "Friend," he asked, "how did you get in here without wedding clothes?" The man was speechless.

'Then the king told the attendants, "Tie him hand and foot, and throw him outside, into the darkness, where there will be weeping and gnashing of teeth."

'For many are invited, but few are chosen.'   MATTHEW 22:2–14

12. The ten virgins

'At that time the kingdom of heaven will be like ten virgins who took their lamps and went out to meet the bridegroom. Five of them were foolish and five were wise. The foolish ones took their lamps but did not take any oil with them. The wise, however, took oil in jars along with their lamps. The bridegroom was a long time in coming, and they all became drowsy and fell asleep.

'At midnight the cry rang out: "Here's the bridegroom! Come out to meet him!"

'Then all the virgins woke up and trimmed their lamps. The foolish ones said to the wise, "Give us some of your oil; our lamps are going out."

'"No," they replied, "there may not be enough for both us and you. Instead, go to those who sell oil and buy some for yourselves."

'But while they were on their way to buy the oil, the bridegroom arrived. The virgins who were ready went in with him to the wedding banquet. And the door was shut.

'Later the others also came. "Sir! Sir!" they said. "Open the door for us!"

'But he replied, "I tell you the truth, I don't know you."

'Therefore keep watch, because you do not know the day or the hour.'   MATTHEW 25:1–13

13. The sheep and the goats

The shepherd separates the sheep from the goats
'When the Son of Man comes in his glory, and all the angels

with him, he will sit on his throne in heavenly glory. All the nations will be gathered before him, and he will separate the people one from another as a shepherd separates the sheep from the goats. He will put the sheep on his right and the goats on his left.'

'I was sick and you looked after me'

'Then the King will say to those on his right, "Come, you who are blessed by my Father; take your inheritance, the kingdom prepared for you since the creation of the world. For I was hungry and you gave me something to eat, I was thirsty and you gave me something to drink, I was a stranger and you invited me in, I needed clothes and you clothed me, I was sick and you looked after me, I was in prison and you came to visit me."

'Then the righteous will answer him, "Lord, when did we see you hungry and feed you, or thirsty and give you something to drink? When did we see you a stranger and invite you in, or needing clothes and clothe you? When did we see you sick or in prison and go to visit you?"

'The King will reply, "I tell you the truth, whatever you did for one of the least of these brothers and sisters of mine, you did for me."'

'I was hungry and you gave me nothing to eat'

'Then he will say to those on his left, "Depart from me, you who are cursed, into the eternal fire prepared for the devil and his angels. For I was hungry and you gave me nothing to eat, I was thirsty and you gave me nothing to drink, I was a stranger and you did not invite me in, I needed clothes and you did not clothe me, I was sick and in prison and you did not look after me."

'They will also answer, "Lord, when did we see you hungry or thirsty or a stranger or needing clothes or sick or in prison, and did not help you?"

'He will reply, "I tell you the truth, whatever you did not do for one of the least of these, you did not do for me."

'Then they will go away to eternal punishment, but the righteous to eternal life.' MATTHEW 25:31–46

14. Using money

While they were listening to this, he went on to tell them a parable, because he was near Jerusalem and the people thought that the kingdom of God was going to appear at once. He said: 'A man of noble birth went to a distant country to have himself appointed king and then to return. So he called ten of his servants and gave them ten minas. "Put this money to work," he said, "until I come back."

'But his subjects hated him and sent a delegation after him to say, "We don't want this man to be our king."

'He was made king, however, and returned home. Then he sent for the servants to whom he had given the money, in order to find out what they had gained with it.'

The first servant
'The first one came and said, "Sir, your mina has earned ten more."

'"Well done, my good servant!" his master replied. "Because you have been trustworthy in a very small matter, take charge of ten cities."'

The second servant
'The second came and said, "Sir, your mina has earned five more."

'His master answered, "You take charge of five cities."'

The third servant
'Then another servant came and said, "Sir, here is your mina; I have kept it laid away in a piece of cloth. I was afraid of you, because you are a hard man. You take out what you did not put in and reap what you did not sow."

'His master replied, "I will judge you by your own words, you wicked servant! You knew, did you, that I am a hard man, taking out what I did not put in, and reaping what I did not sow? Why then didn't you put my money on deposit, so that when I came back, I could have collected it with interest?"

'Then he said to those standing by, "Take his mina away

from him and give it to the one who has ten minas."

'"Sir," they said, "he already has ten!"

'He replied, "I tell you that to everyone who has, more will be given, but as for those who have nothing, even what they have will be taken away. But those enemies of mine who did not want me to be a king over them – bring them here and kill them in front of me."' LUKE 19:11–27

E. Other parables

1. The sower

While a large crowd was gathering and people were coming to Jesus from town after town, he told this parable: 'A farmer went out to sow his seed. As he was scattering the seed, some fell along the path; it was trampled on, and the birds of the air ate it up. Some fell on rock, and when it came up, the plants withered because they had no moisture. Other seed fell among thorns, which grew up with it and choked the plants. Still other seed fell on good soil. It came up and yielded a crop, a hundred times more than was sown.'

When he said this, he called out, 'Those who have ears to hear, let them hear.'

'The seed is the word of God'

'This is the meaning of the parable: The seed is the word of God. Those along the path are the ones who hear, and then the devil comes and takes away the word from their hearts, so that they may not believe and be saved. Those on the rock are the ones who receive the word with joy when they hear it, but they have no root. They believe for a while, but in the time of testing they fall away. The seed that fell among thorns stands for those who hear, but as they go on their way they are choked by life's worries, riches and pleasures, and they do not mature. But the seed on good soil stands for those with a noble and good heart, who hear the word, retain it, and by persevering produce a crop.'   LUKE 8:4–8; 11–15

2. The lost sheep

'Suppose one of you has a hundred sheep and loses one of them. Does he not leave the ninety-nine in the open country and go after the lost sheep until he finds it? And when he finds it, he joyfully puts it on his shoulders and goes home. Then he calls his friends and neighbours together and says, "Rejoice with me; I have found my lost sheep." I tell you that in the same way there will be more rejoicing in heaven over one sinner who repents than over ninety-nine righteous persons who do not need to repent.'   LUKE 15:4–7

3. The lost coin

'Or suppose a woman has ten silver coins and loses one. Does she not light a lamp, sweep the house and search carefully until she finds it? And when she finds it, she calls her friends and neighbours together and says, "Rejoice with me; I have found my lost coin." In the same way, I tell you, there is rejoicing in the presence of the angels of God over one sinner who repents.'   LUKE 15:8–10

4. The runaway son

'Father, give me my share of the estate'

Jesus continued: 'There was a man who had two sons. The younger one said to his father, "Father, give me my share of the estate." So he divided his property between them.

'Not long after that, the younger son got together all he had, set off for a distant country and there squandered his wealth in wild living. After he had spent everything, there was a severe famine in that whole country, and he began to be in need. So he went and hired himself out to a citizen of that country, who sent him to his fields to feed pigs. He longed to fill his stomach with the pods that the pigs were eating, but no-one gave him anything.

'When he came to his senses, he said, "How many of my father's hired servants have food to spare, and here I am starving to death! I will set out and go back to my father and say to him: Father, I have sinned against heaven and against you. I am no longer worthy to be called your son; make me like one of your hired servants."'

The father ran to his son

'So he got up and went to his father.

'But while he was still a long way off, his father saw him and was filled with compassion for him; he ran to his son, threw his arms around him and kissed him.

'The son said to him, "Father, I have sinned against heaven and against you. I am no longer worthy to be called your son."

'But the father said to his servants, "Quick! Bring the best robe and put it on him. Put a ring on his finger and sandals on his feet. Bring the fattened calf and kill it. Let's have a feast and celebrate. For this son of mine was dead and is alive again; he was lost and is found." So they began to celebrate.

'Meanwhile, the older son was in the field. When he came near the house, he heard music and dancing. So he called one of the servants and asked him what was going on. "Your brother has come," he replied, "and your father has killed the fattened calf because he has him back safe and sound."'

'The older brother became angry'

The older brother became angry and refused to go in. So his father went out and pleaded with him. But he answered his father, "Look! All these years I've been slaving for you and never disobeyed your orders. Yet you never gave me even a young goat so I could celebrate with my friends. But when this

son of yours who has squandered your property with prostitutes comes home you kill the fattened calf for him!"'

'We had to celebrate'
'"My son," the father said, "you are always with me, and everything I have is yours. But we had to celebrate and be glad,
because this brother of yours was dead and is alive again; he
was lost and is found."'   LUKE 15:11–32

5. The tenants in the vineyard

'Listen to another parable: There was a landowner who planted
a vineyard. He put a wall around it, dug a winepress in it and
built a watchtower. Then he rented the vineyard to some far-
mers and went away on a journey. When the harvest time
approached, he sent his servants to the tenants to collect his
fruit.

The tenants seized his servants; they beat one, killed
another, and stoned a third. Then he sent other servants to
them, more than the first time, and the tenants treated them
the same way. Last of all, he sent his son to them. "They will
respect my son," he said.'

They killed the son
'But when the tenants saw the son, they said to each other,
"This is the heir. Come, let's kill him and take his inheritance."
So they took him and threw him out of the vineyard and killed
him.

'Therefore, when the owner of the vineyard comes, what will
he do to those tenants?'

'He will bring those wretches to a wretched end,' they
replied, 'and he will rent the vineyard to other tenants, who
will give him his share of the crop at harvest time.'

Jesus said to them, 'Have you never read in the Scriptures:
  '"The stone the builders rejected
    has become the capstone;

the Lord has done this,
      and it is marvellous in our eyes"?
'Therefore I tell you that the kingdom of God will be taken away
from you and given to a people who will produce its fruit. Anyone who falls on this stone will be broken to pieces, but anyone
on whom it falls will be crushed.'

When the chief priests and the Pharisees heard Jesus' parables, they knew he was talking about them. They looked for a
way to arrest him, but they were afraid of the crowd because
the people held that he was a prophet.   MATTHEW 21:33–46

6. 'Who is my neighbour?'

On one occasion an expert in the law stood up to test Jesus.
'Teacher,' he asked, 'what must I do to inherit eternal life?'

'What is written in the Law?' he replied. 'How do you read it?'

He answered: '"Love the Lord your God with all your heart
and with all your soul and with all your strength and with all
your mind"; and, "Love your neighbour as yourself."'

'You have answered correctly,' Jesus replied. 'Do this and
you will live.'

But he wanted to justify himself, so he asked Jesus, 'And who
is my neighbour?'

In reply Jesus said: 'A man was going down from Jerusalem
to Jericho, when he fell into the hands of robbers. They strip-
ped him of his clothes, beat him and went away, leaving him
half-dead.'

The priest and the Levite

'A priest happened to be going down the same road, and when
he saw the man, he passed by on the other side. So too, a
Levite, when he came to the place and saw him, passed by on
the other side.'

When the Samaritan saw him he took pity on him

'But a Samaritan, as he travelled, came where the man was; and when he saw him, he took pity on him. He went to him and bandaged his wounds, pouring on oil and wine. Then he put the man on his own donkey, brought him to an inn and took care of him. The next day he took out two silver coins and gave them to the innkeeper. "Look after him," he said, "and when I return, I will reimburse you for any extra expense you may have."

'Which of these three do you think was a neighbour to the man who fell into the hands of robbers?'

The expert in the law replied, 'The one who had mercy on him.'

Jesus told him, 'Go and do likewise.'   LUKE 10:25–37

7. The rich fool

Someone in the crowd said to him, 'Teacher, tell my brother to divide the inheritance with me.'

Jesus replied, 'Friend, who appointed me a judge or an arbiter between you?' Then he said to them, 'Watch out! Be on your guard against all kinds of greed; life does not consist in the abundance of possessions.'

And he told them this parable: 'The ground of a certain rich man produced a good crop. He thought to himself, "What shall I do? I have no place to store my crops."

'Then he said, "This is what I'll do. I will tear down my barns and build bigger ones, and there I will store all my grain and my goods. And I'll say to myself, 'You have plenty of good things laid up for many years. Take life easy; eat, drink and be merry.'"

'But God said to him, "You fool! This very night your life will be demanded from you. Then who will get what you have prepared for yourself?"

'This is how it will be with those who store up things for themselves but are not rich towards God.'   LUKE 12:13–21

8. Humility and hospitality

When he noticed how the guests picked the places of honour at the table, he told them this parable: 'When someone invites you to a wedding feast, do not take the place of honour, for a person more distinguished than you may have been invited. If so, the host who invited both of you will come and say to you, "Give this person your seat." Then, humiliated, you will have to take the least important place. But when you are invited, take the lowest place, so that when your host comes, he will say to you, "Friend, move up to a better place." Then you will be honoured in the presence of all the other guests. For all those who exalt themselves will be humbled, and those who humble themselves will be exalted.'   LUKE 14:7–11

9. The cost of being a disciple

'Suppose one of you wants to build a tower. Will you not first sit down and estimate the cost to see if you have enough money to complete it? For if you lay the foundation and are not able to finish it, everyone who sees it will ridicule you, saying, "This person began to build and was not able to finish."

'Or suppose a king is about to go to war against another king. Will he not first sit down and consider whether he is able with ten thousand men to oppose the one coming against him with twenty thousand? If he is not able, he will send a delegation while the other is still a long way off and will ask for terms of peace. In the same way, those of you who do not give up everything you have cannot be my disciple.'   LUKE 14:28–33

10. The shrewd manager

Jesus told his disciples: 'There was a rich man whose manager was accused of wasting his possessions. So he called him in and asked him, "What is this I hear about you? Give an account of your management, because you cannot be manager any longer."

'The manager said to himself, "What shall I do now? My

master is taking away my job. I'm not strong enough to dig, and I'm ashamed to beg – I know what I'll do so that, when I lose my job here, people will welcome me into their houses."

'So he called in each one of his master's debtors. He asked the first, "How much do you owe my master?"

'"Eight hundred gallons of olive oil," he replied.

'The manager told him, "Take your bill, sit down quickly, and make it four hundred."

'Then he asked the second, "And how much do you owe?"

'"A thousand bushels of wheat," he replied.

'He told him, "Take your bill and make it eight hundred."

'The master commended the dishonest manager because he had acted shrewdly. For the people of this world are more shrewd in dealing with their own kind than are the people of the light. I tell you, use worldly wealth to gain friends for yourselves, so that when it is gone, you will be welcomed into eternal dwellings.

'Whoever can be trusted with very little can also be trusted with much, and whoever is dishonest with very little will also be dishonest with much. So if you have not been trustworthy in handling worldly wealth, who will trust you with true riches? And if you have not been trustworthy with someone else's property, who will give you property of your own?'   LUKE 16:1–12

11. The rich man and Lazarus

'There was a rich man who was dressed in purple and fine linen and lived in luxury every day. At his gate was laid a beggar named Lazarus, covered with sores and longing to eat what fell from the rich man's table. Even the dogs came and licked his sores.

'The time came when the beggar died and the angels carried him to Abraham's side. The rich man also died and was buried. In hell, where he was in torment, he looked up and saw Abraham far away, with Lazarus by his side. So he called to him, "Father Abraham, have pity on me and send Lazarus to dip the tip of his finger in water and cool my tongue, because I am in agony in this fire."

'But Abraham replied, "Son, remember that in your lifetime you received your good things, while Lazarus received bad things, but now he is comforted here and you are in agony. And besides all this, between us and you a great chasm has been fixed, so that those who want to go from here to you cannot, nor can anyone cross over from there to us."

'He answered, "Then I beg you, father, send Lazarus to my father's house, for I have five brothers. Let him warn them, so that they will not also come to this place of torment."

'Abraham replied, "They have Moses and the Prophets; let them listen to them."

'"No, father Abraham," he said, "but if someone from the dead goes to them, they will repent."

'He said to him, "If they do not listen to Moses and the Prophets, they will not be convinced even if someone rises from the dead."'   LUKE 16:19–31

12. The Pharisee and the tax collector

To some who were confident of their own righteousness and looked down on everybody else, Jesus told this parable: 'Two men went up to the temple to pray, one a Pharisee and the other a tax collector. The Pharisee stood up and prayed about himself: "God, I thank you that I am not like other men – robbers, evildoers, adulterers – or even like this tax collector. I fast twice a week and give a tenth of all I get."

'But the tax collector stood at a distance. He would not even look up to heaven, but beat his breast and said, "God, have mercy on me, a sinner."

'I tell you that this man, rather than the other, went home justified before God. For all those who exalt themselves will be humbled, and those who humble themselves will be exalted.'   LUKE 18:9–14

13. The great banquet

When one of those at the table with him heard this, he said to Jesus, 'Blessed is the one who will eat at the feast in the kingdom of God.'

Jesus replied, 'A certain man was preparing a great banquet and invited many guests. At the time of the banquet he sent his servant to tell those who had been invited, "Come, for everything is now ready."

'But they all alike began to make excuses. The first said, "I have just bought a field and I must go and see it. Please excuse me."

'Another said, "I have just bought five yoke of oxen, and I'm on my way to try them out. Please excuse me."

'Still another said, "I have just got married, so I can't come."

'The servant came back and reported this to his master. Then the owner of the house became angry and ordered his servant, "Go out quickly into the streets and alleys of the town and bring in the poor, the crippled, the blind and the lame."

'"Sir," the servant said, "what you ordered has been done, but there is still room."

'Then the master told his servant, "Go out to the roads and country lanes and make them come in, so that my house will be full. I tell you, not one of those who were invited will get a taste of my banquet."' LUKE 14:15–24

14. The purpose of the parables

His disciples asked him what this parable meant. He said, 'The knowledge of the secrets of the kingdom of God has been given to you, but to others I speak in parables, so that,

'"though seeing, they may not see;
    though hearing, they may not understand."' LUKE 8:9–10

F. The future

1. 'A hundred times as much'

Peter answered him, 'We have left everything to follow you! What then will there be for us?'

Jesus said to them, 'I tell you the truth, at the renewal of all things, when the Son of Man sits on his glorious throne, you who have followed me will also sit on twelve thrones, judging the twelve tribes of Israel. And everyone who has left houses or brothers or sisters or father or mother or children or fields for my sake will receive a hundred times as much and will inherit eternal life. But many who are first will be last, and many who are last will be first.'   MATTHEW 19:27–30

2. 'Destroy this temple . . .'

Then the Jews demanded of him, 'What miraculous sign can you show us to prove your authority to do all this?'

Jesus answered them, 'Destroy this temple, and I will raise it again in three days.'

The Jews replied, 'It has taken forty-six years to build this temple, and you are going to raise it in three days?' But the temple he had spoken of was his body. After he was raised from the dead, his disciples recalled what he had said. Then they believed the Scripture and the words that Jesus had spoken.
JOHN 2:18–22

3. Signs of the end of the age

'Not one stone here will be left on another'
Jesus left the temple and was walking away when his disciples came up to him to call his attention to its buildings. 'Do you see all these things?' he asked. 'I tell you the truth, not one

stone here will be left on another; every one will be thrown down.'

As Jesus was sitting on the Mount of Olives, the disciples came to him privately. 'Tell us,' they said, 'when will this happen, and what will be the sign of your coming and of the end of the age?' MATTHEW 24:1–3

Troubles and persecutions

Jesus answered, 'Watch out that no-one deceives you. For many will come in my name, claiming, "I am the Christ," and will deceive many. You will hear of wars and rumours of wars, but see to it that you are not alarmed. Such things must happen, but the end is still to come. Nation will rise against nation, and kingdom against kingdom. There will be famines and earthquakes in various places. All these are the beginning of birthpains.

'Then you will be handed over to be persecuted and put to death, and you will be hated by all nations because of me. At that time many will turn away from the faith and will betray and hate each other, and many false prophets will appear and deceive many people. Because of the increase of wickedness, the love of most will grow cold, but whoever stands firm to the end will be saved. And this gospel of the kingdom will be preached in the whole world as a testimony to all nations, and then the end will come.' MATTHEW 24:4–14

'The abomination that causes desolation'

'So when you see standing in the holy place "the abomination that causes desolation", spoken of through the prophet Daniel – let the reader understand – then let those who are in Judea flee to the mountains. Let no-one on the housetop go down to take anything out of the house. Let no-one in the field go back to get a cloak. How dreadful it will be in those days for pregnant women and nursing mothers! Pray that your flight will not take place in winter or on the Sabbath. For then there will be great distress, unequalled from the beginning of the world until now – and never to be equalled again. If those days had not been cut short, no-one would survive, but for the sake of the elect those days will be shortened. At that time if anyone says to you, "Look, here is the Christ!" or, "There he is!" do not believe it. For false Christs and false prophets will appear and perform great signs and miracles to deceive even the elect – if that were possible. See, I have told you ahead of time.

'So if anyone tells you, "There he is, out in the desert," do not go out; or, "Here he is, in the inner rooms," do not believe it. For as lightning that comes from the east is visible even in the west, so will be the coming of the Son of Man. Wherever there is a carcass, there the vultures will gather.'   MATTHEW 24:15–28

The coming of the Son of Man
'Immediately after the distress of those days

'"the sun will be darkened,
  and the moon will not give its light;
 the stars will fall from the sky,
  and the heavenly bodies will be shaken."

'At that time the sign of the Son of Man will appear in the sky, and all the nations of the earth will mourn. They will see the Son of Man coming on the clouds of the sky, with power and great glory. And he will send his angels with a loud trumpet call, and they will gather his elect from the four winds, from one end of the heavens to the other.'   MATTHEW 24:29–31

Jesus must suffer first
Then he said to his disciples, 'The time is coming when you will long to see one of the days of the Son of Man, but you will not see it. Men will tell you, "There he is!" or "Here he is!" Do not go running off after them. For the Son of Man in his day will be like the lightning, which flashes and lights up the sky from one end to the other. But first he must suffer many things and be rejected by this generation.'   LUKE 17:22–25

The lesson of the fig-tree
'Now learn this lesson from the fig-tree: As soon as its twigs get tender and its leaves come out, you know that summer is near.

Even so, when you see all these things, you know that it is near, right at the door. I tell you the truth, this generation will certainly not pass away until all these things have happened. Heaven and earth will pass away, but my words will never pass away.'   MATTHEW 24:32-35

'Remember Lot's wife!'

'On that day no-one who is on the top of the house, with goods inside, should go down to get them. Likewise, no-one in the field should go back for anything. Remember Lot's wife! Those who try to keep their lives will lose them, and those who lose their lives will preserve them. . . .'

'Where, Lord?' they asked.

He replied, 'Where there is a dead body, there the vultures will gather.'   LUKE 17:31-33, 37

The day and hour unknown

'No-one knows about that day or hour, not even the angels in heaven, nor the Son, but only the Father. As it was in the days of Noah, so it will be at the coming of the Son of Man. For in the days before the flood, people were eating and drinking, marrying and giving in marriage, up to the day Noah entered the ark; and they knew nothing about what would happen until the flood came and took them all away. That is how it will be at the coming of the Son of Man. Two men will be in the field; one will be taken and the other left. Two women will be grinding with a hand mill; one will be taken and the other left.

'Therefore keep watch, because you do not know on what day your Lord will come. But understand this: If the owner of the house had known at what time of night the thief was coming, he would have kept watch and would not have let his house be broken into. So you also must be ready, because the Son of Man will come at an hour when you do not expect him.'
MATTHEW 24:36-44

Watchful servants

'Be dressed ready for service and keep your lamps burning, like those waiting for their master to return from a wedding banquet, so that when he comes and knocks they can immediately open the door for him. It will be good for those servants whose master finds them watching when he comes. I tell you the truth, he will dress himself to serve, will have them recline at the table and will come and wait on them. It will be good for those servants whose master finds them ready, even if he comes in the second or third watch of the night. But understand this: If the owner of the house had known at what hour the thief was coming, he would not have let his house be broken into. You also must be ready, because the Son of Man will come at an hour when you do not expect him.'   LUKE 12:35–40

The faithful servant
'Who then is the faithful and wise servant, whom the master has put in charge of the servants in his household to give them their food at the proper time? It will be good for that servant whose master finds him doing so when he returns. I tell you the truth, he will put him in charge of all his possessions. But suppose that servant is wicked and says to himself, "My master is staying away a long time," and he then begins to beat his fellow servants and to eat and drink with drunkards. The master of that servant will come on a day when he does not expect him and at an hour he is not aware of. He will cut him to pieces and assign him a place with the hypocrites, where there will be weeping and gnashing of teeth.'   MATTHEW 24:45–51

G. Teaching about himself

1. The seven 'I am's'

'I am the bread of life'
Then Jesus declared, 'I am the bread of life. Whoever comes to me will never go hungry, and whoever believes in me will never

be thirsty. But as I told you, you have seen me and still you do not believe. All that the Father gives me will come to me, and whoever comes to me I will never drive away. For I have come down from heaven not to do my will but to do the will of him who sent me. And this is the will of him who sent me, that I shall lose none of all that he has given me, but raise them up at the last day. For my Father's will is that all those who look to the Son and believe in him shall have eternal life, and I will raise them up at the last day.'   JOHN 6:35–40

'I am the light of the world'

When Jesus spoke again to the people, he said, 'I am the light of the world. Whoever follows me will never walk in darkness, but will have the light of life.'

The Pharisees challenged him, 'Here you are, appearing as your own witness; your testimony is not valid.'

Jesus answered, 'Even if I testify on my own behalf, my testimony is valid, for I know where I came from and where I am going. But you have no idea where I come from or where I am going. You judge by human standards; I pass judgment on noone. But if I do judge, my decisions are right, because I am not alone. I stand with the Father who sent me. In your own Law it is written that the testimony of two witnesses is valid. I am one who testifies for myself; my other witness is the Father who sent me.'

Then they asked him, 'Where is your father?'

'You do not know me or my Father,' Jesus replied. 'If you knew me, you would know my Father also.'   JOHN 8:12–19

'I am the gate for the sheep'

'I tell you the truth, anyone who does not enter the sheep pen by the gate, but climbs in by some other way, is a thief and a robber. The one who enters by the gate is the shepherd of his sheep. The gatekeeper opens the gate for him, and the sheep listen to his voice. He calls his own sheep by name and leads them out. When he has brought out all his own, he goes on ahead of them, and his sheep follow him because they know his voice. But they will never follow a stranger; in fact, they will run away from him because they do not recognise a stranger's voice.' Jesus used this figure of speech, but they did not understand what he was telling them.

Therefore Jesus said again, 'I tell you the truth, I am the gate for the sheep. All who ever came before me were thieves and robbers, but the sheep did not listen to them. I am the gate; all who enter through me will be saved. They will come in and go out, and find pasture. The thief comes only to steal and kill and destroy; I have come that they may have life, and have it to the full.'   JOHN 10:1–10

'I am the good shepherd'

'I am the good shepherd. The good shepherd lays down his life for the sheep. The hired hand is not the shepherd who owns the sheep. So when he sees the wolf coming, he abandons the sheep and runs away. Then the wolf attacks the flock and scatters it. The man runs away because he is a hired hand and cares nothing for the sheep.

'I am the good shepherd; I know my sheep and my sheep know me – just as the Father knows me and I know the father – and I lay down my life for the sheep. I have other sheep that are not of this sheep pen. I must bring them also. They too will listen to my voice, and there shall be one flock and one shepherd. The reason my Father loves me is that I lay down my life – only to take it up again. No-one takes it from me, but I lay it down of my own accord. I have authority to lay it down and authority to take it up again. This command I received from my Father.'   JOHN 10:11–18

'I am the resurrection and the life'

'Lord,' Martha said to Jesus, 'if you had been here, my brother would not have died. But I know that even now God will give you whatever you ask.'

Jesus said to her, 'Your brother will rise again.'

Martha answered, 'I know he will rise again in the resurrection at the last day.'

Jesus said to her, 'I am the resurrection and the life. Those who believe in me will live, even though they die; and whoever lives and believes in me will never die. Do you believe this?' . . .

When Mary reached the place where Jesus was and saw him, she fell at his feet and said, 'Lord, if you had been here, my brother would not have died.'

When Jesus saw her weeping, and the Jews who had come along with her also weeping, he was deeply moved in spirit and troubled. 'Where have you laid him?' he asked.

'Come and see, Lord,' they replied.

Jesus wept.

Then the Jews said, 'See how he loved him!'

But some of them said, 'Could not he who opened the eyes of the blind man have kept this man from dying?'

Jesus, once more deeply moved, came to the tomb. It was a cave with a stone laid across the entrance. 'Take away the stone,' he said.

'But Lord,' said Martha, the sister of the dead man, 'by this time there is a bad odour, for he has been there four days.'

Then Jesus said, 'Did I not tell you that if you believed, you would see the glory of God?'

So they took away the stone. Then Jesus looked up and said, 'Father, I thank you that you have heard me. I knew that you always hear me, but I said this for the benefit of the people standing here, that they may believe that you sent me.'

When he had said this, Jesus called in a loud voice, 'Lazarus, come out!' The dead man came out, his hands and feet wrapped with strips of linen, and a cloth around his face.

Jesus said to them, 'Take off the grave clothes and let him go.' JOHN 11:21–26; 32–44

'I am the way – and the truth and the life'

'Do not let your hearts be troubled. Trust in God; trust also in me. In my Father's house are many rooms; if it were not so, I would have told you. I am going there to prepare a place for you. And if I go and prepare a place for you, I will come back and take you to be with me that you also may be where I am.

You know the way to the place where I am going.'

Thomas said to him, 'Lord, we don't know where you are going, so how can we know the way?'

Jesus answered, 'I am the way and the truth and the life. No-one comes to the Father except through me.'   JOHN 14:1–6

'I am the true vine'

'I am the true vine and my Father is the gardener. He cuts off every branch in me that bears no fruit, while every branch that does bear fruit he prunes so that it will be even more fruitful. You are already clean because of the word I have spoken to you. Remain in me, and I will remain in you. No branch can bear fruit by itself; it must remain in the vine. Neither can you bear fruit unless you remain in me.

'I am the vine; you are the branches. If you remain in me and I in you, you will bear much fruit; apart from me you can do nothing. If you do not remain in me, you are like a branch that is thrown away and withers; such branches are picked up, thrown into the fire and burned. If you remain in me and my words remain in you, ask whatever you wish, and it will be given you. This is to my Father's glory, that you bear much fruit, showing yourselves to be my disciples.

'As the Father has loved me, so have I loved you. Now remain in my love. If you obey my commands, you will remain in my love, just as I have obeyed my Father's commands and remain in his love.'   JOHN 15:1–10

❧ WORDS OF THE RISEN LORD ❧

A. To the apostle Paul

1. At Paul's conversion

'Saul! Saul! Why do you persecute me?'
'About noon as I came near Damascus, suddenly a bright light from heaven flashed around me. I fell to the ground and heard a voice say to me, "Saul! Saul! Why do you persecute me?"

'"Who are you, Lord?" I asked.

'"I am Jesus of Nazareth, whom you are persecuting," he replied. My companions saw the light, but they did not understand the voice of him who was speaking to me.

'"What shall I do, Lord?" I asked.

'"Get up," the Lord said, "and go into Damascus. There you will be told all that you have been assigned to do."' ACTS 22:6–10

'I have appeared to you to appoint you as a witness'
'Then I asked, "Who are you, Lord?"

'"I am Jesus, whom you are persecuting," the Lord replied. "Now get up and stand on your feet. I have appeared to you to appoint you as a servant and as a witness of what you have seen of me and what I will show you. I will rescue you from your own people and from the Gentiles. I am sending you to them to open their eyes and turn them from darkness to light, and from the power of Satan to God, so that they may receive forgiveness of sins and a place among those who are sanctified by faith in me."' ACTS 26:15–18

'Ananias, enquire for a man named Saul'
In Damascus there was a disciple named Ananias. The Lord called to him in a vision, 'Ananias!'

'Yes, Lord,' he answered.

The Lord told him, 'Go to the house of Judas on Straight Street and ask for a man from Tarsus named Saul, for he is praying. In a vision he has seen a man named Ananias come and place his hands on him to restore his sight.'

'Lord,' Ananias answered, 'I have heard many reports about this man and all the harm he has done to your saints in Jerusalem. And he has come here with authority from the chief priests to arrest all who call on your name.'

But the Lord said to Ananias, 'Go! This man is my chosen instrument to carry my name before the Gentiles and their kings and before the people of Israel. I will show him how much he must suffer for my name.'   ACTS 9:10–16

2. The risen Jesus answers Paul's prayer

To keep me from becoming conceited because of these surpassingly great revelations, there was given me a thorn in my flesh, a messenger of Satan, to torment me. Three times I pleaded with the Lord to take it away from me. But he said to me, 'My grace is sufficient for you, for my power is made perfect in weakness.' Therefore I will boast all the more gladly about my weaknesses, so that Christ's power may rest on me.   2 CORINTHIANS 12:7–9

3. The risen Jesus stood by Paul

The dispute became so violent that the commander was afraid Paul would be torn to pieces by them. He ordered the troops to go down and take him away from them by force and bring him into the barracks.

The following night the Lord stood near Paul and said, 'Take courage! As you have testified about me in Jerusalem, so you must also testify in Rome.'   ACTS 23:10–11

B. In the book of Revelation

1. Words to the seven churches

To the church at Ephesus
'I hold this against you: You have forsaken your first love. Remember the height from which you have fallen! Repent and do the things you did at first. If you do not repent, I will come to you and remove your lampstand from its place.'   REVELATION 2:4–5

To the church at Smyrna
'Do not be afraid of what you are about to suffer. I tell you, the devil will put some of you in prison to test you, and you will suffer persecution for ten days. Be faithful, even to the point of death, and I will give you the crown of life.'   REVELATION 2:10

To the church at Pergamum
'I have a few things against you: You have people there who hold to the teaching of Balaam, who taught Balak to entice the Israelites to sin by eating food sacrificed to idols and by committing sexual immorality.'   REVELATION 2:14

To the church at Thyatira
'I know your deeds, your love and faith, your service and perseverance, and that you are now doing more than you did at first.

'Nevertheless, I have this against you: You tolerate that woman Jezebel, who calls herself a prophetess. By her teaching she misleads my servants into sexual immorality and the eating of food sacrificed to idols . . . Hold on to what you have until I come.'   REVELATION 2:19–20; 25

To the church at Sardis
'Wake up! Strengthen what remains and is about to die, for I have not found your deeds complete in the sight of my God. Remember, therefore, what you have received and heard; obey it, and repent. But if you do not wake up, I will come like a

thief, and you will not know at what time I will come to you.'   REVELATION 3:2–3

To the church at Philadelphia
'Since you have kept my command to endure patiently, I will also keep you from the hour of trial that is going to come upon the whole world to test those who live on the earth.

'I am coming soon. Hold on to what you have, so that no-one will take your crown. Those who overcome I will make pillars in the temple of my God. Never again will they leave it. I will write on them the name of my God and the name of the city of my God, the new Jerusalem, which is coming down out of heaven from my God; and I will also write on them my new name.'   REVELATION 3:10–12

To the church at Laodicea
'I know your deeds, that you are neither cold nor hot. I wish you were either one or the other! So, because you are lukewarm – neither hot nor cold – I am about to spit you out of my mouth. You say, "I am rich; I have acquired wealth and do not need a thing." But you do not realise that you are wretched, pitiful, poor, blind and naked. I counsel you to buy from me gold refined in the fire, so that you can become rich; and white clothes to wear, so that you can cover your shameful naked-ness; and salve to put on your eyes, so that you can see.

'Those whom I love I rebuke and discipline. So be earnest, and repent. Here I am! I stand at the door and knock. If anyone hears my voice and opens the door, I will come in and eat with them, and they with me.

'To those who overcome, I will give the right to sit with me on my throne, just as I overcame and sat down with my Father on his throne.'   REVELATION 3:15–21

2. 'I am coming soon'

'Behold, I am coming soon! Blessed are those who keep the

words of the prophecy in this book.

'Behold, I am coming soon! My reward is with me, and I will give to everyone according to what they have done.

'I Jesus, have sent my angel to give you this testimony for the churches. I am the Root and the Offspring of David, and the bright Morning Star.'

He who testifies to these things says, 'Yes, I am coming soon.'

Amen. Come, Lord Jesus.   REVELATION 22:7, 12, 16, 20

PART 2

WHAT JESUS DID

⤳ THE LIFE OF JESUS ⤳

A. Youth

1. The twelve-year-old Jesus in the temple

After three days they found him in the temple courts, sitting among the teachers, listening to them and asking them questions. Everyone who heard him was amazed at his understanding and his answers. When his parents saw him, they were astonished. His mother said to him, 'Son, why have you treated us like this? Your father and I have been anxiously searching for you.'

'Why were you searching for me?' he asked. 'Didn't you know I had to be in my Father's house?'   LUKE 2:46–49

B. Public ministry

1. The baptism of Jesus

Then Jesus came from Galilee to the Jordan to be baptised by John. But John tried to deter him, saying, 'I need to be baptised by you, and do you come to me?'

Jesus replied, 'Let it be so now; it is proper for us to do this to fulfil all righteousness.' Then John consented.

As soon as Jesus was baptised, he went up out of the water. At that moment heaven was opened, and he saw the Spirit of God descending like a dove and lighting on him. And a voice from heaven said, 'This is my Son, whom I love; with him I am well pleased.'   MATTHEW 3:13–17

2. Jesus is tempted

Then Jesus was led by the Spirit into the desert to be tempted by the devil. After fasting for forty days and forty nights, he was hungry. The tempter came to him and said, 'If you are the Son of God, tell these stones to become bread.'

Jesus answered, 'It is written: "People do not live on bread alone, but on every word that comes from the mouth of God."'

Then the devil took him to the holy city and had him stand on the highest point of the temple. 'If you are the Son of God,' he said, 'throw yourself down. For it is written:

'"He will command his angels concerning you,
   and they will lift you up in their hands,
so that you will not strike your foot against a stone."'

Jesus answered him, 'It is also written: "Do not put the Lord your God to the test."'

Again, the devil took him to a very high mountain and showed him all the kingdoms of the world and their splendour. 'All this I will give you,' he said, 'if you will bow down and worship me.'

Jesus said to him, 'Away from me, Satan! For it is written: "Worship the Lord your God, and serve him only."'

Then the devil left him, and angels came and attended him.   MATTHEW 4:1–11

3. Jesus preaches in Galilee

After John was put in prison, Jesus went into Galilee, proclaiming the good news of God. 'The time has come,' he said. 'The kingdom of God is near. Repent and believe the good news!'   MARK 1:14–15

4. Jesus travels throughout Galilee

Jesus replied, 'Let us go somewhere else – to the nearby villages

– so that I can preach there also. That is why I have come.' So he travelled throughout Galilee, preaching in their synagogues and driving out demons.   MARK 1:38–39

5. The twelve disciples are given authority over evil spirits and disease

He called his twelve disciples to him and gave them authority to drive out evil spirits and to heal every disease and sickness.

These are the names of the twelve apostles: first, Simon (who is called Peter) and his brother Andrew; James son of Zebedee, and his brother John; Philip and Bartholomew; Thomas and Matthew the tax collector; James son of Alphaeus, and Thaddaeus; Simon the Zealot and Judas Iscariot, who betrayed him.   MATTHEW 10:1–4

6. Jesus sends out seventy-two disciples

After this the Lord appointed seventy-two others and sent them two by two ahead of him to every town and place where he was about to go. He told them, 'The harvest is plentiful, but the workers are few. Ask the Lord of the harvest, therefore, to send out workers into his harvest field. Go! I am sending you out like lambs among wolves. Do not take a purse or bag or sandals; and do not greet anyone on the road.

'When you enter a house, first say, "Peace to this house." If anyone there loves peace, your peace will rest on that person; if not, it will return to you. Stay in that house, eating and drinking whatever they give you, for workers deserve their wages. Do not move around from house to house.

'When you enter a town and are welcomed, eat what is set before you. Heal the sick who are there and tell them, "The kingdom of God is near you."   LUKE 10:1–9

7. The seventy-two disciples return

The seventy-two returned with joy and said, 'Lord, even the demons submit to us in your name.'

He replied, 'I saw Satan fall like lightning from heaven. I have given you authority to trample on snakes and scorpions and to overcome all the power of the enemy; nothing will harm you. However, do not rejoice that the spirits submit to you, but rejoice that your names are written in heaven.'

... Then he turned to his disciples and said privately, 'Blessed are the eyes that see what you see. For I tell you that many prophets and kings wanted to see what you see but did not see it, and to hear what you hear but did not hear it.'   LUKE 10:17–20; 23–24

8. Jesus predicts his death

'Now my heart is troubled, and what shall I say? "Father, save me from this hour"? No, it was for this very reason I came to this hour. Father, glorify your name!'

Then a voice came from heaven, 'I have glorified it, and will glorify it again.' The crowd that was there and heard it said it had thundered; others said an angel had spoken to him.

Jesus said, 'This voice was for your benefit, not mine. Now is the time for judgment on this world; now the prince of this world will be driven out. But I, when I am lifted up from the earth, will draw all men to myself.' He said this to show the kind of death he was going to die.

The crowd spoke up. 'We have heard from the Law that the Christ will remain for ever, so how can you say, "The Son of Man must be lifted up"? Who is this "Son of Man"?'

Then Jesus told them, 'You are going to have the light just a little while longer. Walk while you have the light, before darkness overtakes you. Those who walk in the dark do not know where they are going. Put your trust in the light while you have it, so that you may become children of light.' When he had finished speaking, Jesus left and hid himself from them.   JOHN 12:27–36

9. Jesus is transfigured

After six days Jesus took with him Peter, James and John the brother of James, and led them up a high mountain by themselves. There he was transfigured before them. His face shone like the sun, and his clothes became as white as the light. Just then there appeared before them Moses and Elijah, talking with Jesus.

Peter said to Jesus, 'Lord, it is good for us to be here. If you wish, I will put up three shelters – one for you, one for Moses and one for Elijah.'

While he was still speaking, a bright cloud enveloped them, and a voice from the cloud said, 'This is my Son, whom I love; with him I am well pleased. Listen to him!'

When the disciples heard this, they fell face down to the ground, terrified. But Jesus came and touched them. 'Get up,' he said. 'Don't be afraid.' When they looked up, they saw no-one except Jesus.   MATTHEW 17:1–8

C. Last week

1. Palm Sunday

After Jesus had said this, he went on ahead, going up to Jerusalem. As he approached Bethphage and Bethany at the hill called the Mount of Olives, he sent two of his disciples, saying to them, 'Go to the village ahead of you, and as you enter it, you will find a colt tied there, which no-one has ever ridden. Untie it and bring it here. If anyone asks you, "Why are you untying it?" say, "The Lord needs it."'

Those who were sent ahead went and found it just as he had told them. As they were untying the colt, its owners asked them, 'Why are you untying the colt?'

They replied, 'The Lord needs it.'

They brought it to Jesus, threw their cloaks on the colt and put Jesus on it. As he went along, people spread their cloaks on the road.

When he came near the place where the road goes down the Mount of Olives, the whole crowd of disciples began joyfully to praise God in loud voices for all the miracles they had seen:

'Blessed is the king who comes in the name of the Lord!'

'Peace in heaven and glory in the highest!'

Some of the Pharisees in the crowd said to Jesus, 'Teacher, rebuke your disciples!'

'I tell you,' he replied, 'if they keep quiet, the stones will cry out.'   LUKE 19:28–40

2. Jesus curses the fig-tree

The next day as they were leaving Bethany, Jesus was hungry. Seeing in the distance a fig-tree in leaf, he went to find out if it had any fruit. When he reached it, he found nothing but leaves, because it was not the season for figs. Then he said to the tree, 'May no-one ever eat fruit from you again.' And his disciples heard him say it.

In the morning, as they went along, they saw the fig-tree withered from the roots. Peter remembered and said to Jesus, 'Rabbi, look! The fig-tree you cursed has withered!'

'Have faith in God,' Jesus answered. 'I tell you the truth, if you say to this mountain, 'Go, throw yourself into the sea,' and do not doubt in your heart but believe that what you say will happen, it will be done for you. Therefore I tell you, whatever you ask for in prayer, believe that you have received it, and it will be yours. And when you stand praying, if you hold anything against anyone, forgive them, so that your Father in heaven may forgive you your sins.'   MARK 11:12–14; 20–25

3. Jesus weeps over Jerusalem

As he approached Jerusalem and saw the city, he wept over it and said, 'If you, even you, had only known on this day what would bring you peace – but now it is hidden from your eyes. The days will come upon you when your enemies will build an embankment against you and encircle you and hem you in on every side. They will dash you to the ground, you and the children within your walls. They will not leave one stone on another, because you did not recognise the time of God's coming to you.'   LUKE 19:41–44

4. Jesus clears the temple

When it was almost time for the Jewish Passover, Jesus went up to Jerusalem. In the temple courts he found people selling cattle, sheep and doves, and others sitting at tables exchanging money. So he made a whip out of cords, and drove all from the temple area, both sheep and cattle; he scattered the coins of the money-changers and overturned their tables. To those who sold doves he said, 'Get these out of here! How dare you turn my Father's house into a market!'

His disciples remembered that it is written, 'Zeal for your house will consume me.'   JOHN 2:13–17

D. Last meal

1. A secret sign

Then came the day of Unleavened Bread on which the Passover lamb had to be sacrificed. Jesus sent Peter and John, saying, 'Go and make preparations for us to eat the Passover.'

'Where do you want us to prepare for it?' they asked.

He replied, 'As you enter the city, a man carrying a jar of water will meet you. Follow him to the house that he enters, and say to the owner of the house, "The Teacher asks: Where is the guest room, where I may eat the Passover with my disciples?" He will show you a large upper room, all furnished. Make preparations there.'

They left and found things just as Jesus had told them. So they prepared the Passover. LUKE 22:7-13

2. The Passover meal

When evening came, Jesus was reclining at the table with the Twelve. And while they were eating, he said, 'I tell you the truth, one of you will betray me.'

They were very sad and began to say to him one after the other, 'Surely not I, Lord?'

Jesus replied, 'The one who has dipped his hand into the bowl with me will betray me. The Son of Man will go just as it is written about him. But woe to that man who betrays the Son of Man! It would be better for him if he had not been born.'

Then Judas, the one who would betray him, said, 'Surely not I, Rabbi?'

Jesus answered, 'Yes, it is you.' MATTHEW 26:20-25

3. Jesus washes the disciples' feet

The evening meal was being served, and the devil had already prompted Judas Iscariot, son of Simon, to betray Jesus. Jesus knew that the Father had put all things under his power, and that he had come from God and was returning to God; so he got up from the meal, took off his outer clothing, and wrapped a towel round his waist. After that, he poured water into a basin and began to wash his disciples' feet, drying them with the towel that was wrapped round him.

He came to Simon Peter, who said to him, 'Lord, are you going to wash my feet?' Jesus replied, 'You do not realise now what I am doing, but later you will understand.'

'No,' said Peter, 'you shall never wash my feet.'

Jesus answered, 'Unless I wash you, you have no part with me.'

'Then, Lord,' Simon Peter replied, 'not just my feet but my hands and my head as well!'

Jesus answered, 'Those who have had a bath need only to wash their feet; their whole body is clean. And you are clean, though not every one of you.' For he knew who was going to betray him, and that was why he said not every one was clean.

When he had finished washing their feet, he put on his clothes and returned to his place. 'Do you understand what I have done for you?' he asked them. 'You call me "Teacher" and "Lord", and rightly so, for that is what I am. Now that I, your Lord and Teacher, have washed your feet, you also should wash one another's feet. I have set you an example that you should do as I have done for you. I tell you the truth, servants are not greater than their masters, nor are messengers greater than those who sent them. Now that you know these things, you will be blessed if you do them.

'I am not referring to all of you; I know those I have chosen. But this is to fulfil the scripture: "He who shares my bread has lifted up his heel against me."

I am telling you now before it happens, so that when it does happen you will believe that I am He. I tell you the truth, whoever accepts anyone I send accepts me; and whoever accepts me accepts the one who sent me.' JOHN 13:2–20

4. The Last Supper

When the hour came, Jesus and his apostles reclined at the table. And he said to them, 'I have eagerly desired to eat this Passover with you before I suffer. For I tell you, I will not eat it again until it finds fulfilment in the kingdom of God.'

After taking the cup, he gave thanks and said, 'Take this and divide it among you. For I tell you I will not drink again of the fruit of the vine until the kingdom of God comes.'

And he took bread, gave thanks and broke it, and gave it to them, saying, 'This is my body given for you; do this in remembrance of me.'

In the same way, after the supper he took the cup, saying, 'This cup is the new covenant in my blood, which is poured out for you. But the hand of him who is going to betray me is with mine on the table. The Son of Man will go as it has been decreed, but woe to that man who betrays him.' They began to question among themselves which of them it might be who would do this.   LUKE 22:14–23

5. Paul's record of the Lord's Supper

For I received from the Lord what I also passed on to you: The Lord Jesus, on the night he was betrayed, took bread, and when he had given thanks, he broke it and said, 'This is my body, which is for you; do this in remembrance of me.' In the same way, after supper he took the cup, saying, 'This cup is the new covenant in my blood; do this, whenever you drink it, in remembrance of me.' For whenever you eat this bread and drink this cup, you proclaim the Lord's death until he comes.   1 CORINTHIANS 11:23–26

6. Jesus predicts Peter's denial

Then Jesus told them, 'This very night you will all fall away on account of me, for it is written:
  '"I will strike the shepherd,
    and the sheep of the flock will be scattered."'
But after I have risen, I will go ahead of you into Galilee.'

Peter replied, 'Even if all fall away on account of you, I never will.'

'I tell you the truth,' Jesus answered, 'this very night, before the cock crows, you will disown me three times.'

But Peter declared, 'Even if I have to die with you, I will never disown you.' And all the other disciples said the same.   MATTHEW 26:31–35

7. Jesus predicts his betrayal

After he had said this Jesus was troubled in spirit and testified, 'I tell you the truth, one of you is going to betray me.'

His disciples stared at one another, at a loss to know which of them he meant. One of them, the disciple whom Jesus loved, was reclining next to him. Simon Peter motioned to this disciple and said, 'Ask him which one he means.'

Leaning back against Jesus, he asked him, 'Lord, who is it?'

Jesus answered, 'It is the one to whom I will give this piece of bread when I have dipped it in the dish.' Then, dipping the piece of bread, he gave it to Judas Iscariot, son of Simon. As soon as Judas took the bread, Satan entered into him.

'What you are about to do, do quickly,' Jesus told him, but no-one at the meal understood why Jesus said this to him. Since Judas had charge of the money, some thought Jesus was telling him to buy what was needed for the Feast, or to give something to the poor. As soon as Judas had taken the bread, he went out. And it was night.   JOHN 13:21–30

8. Jesus gives a new commandment

When he was gone, Jesus said, 'Now is the Son of Man glorified and God is glorified in him. If God is glorified in him, God will glorify the Son in himself, and will glorify him at once.

'My children, I will be with you only a little longer. You will look for me, and just as I told the Jews, so I tell you now: Where I am going, you cannot come.

'A new command I give you: Love one another. As I have loved you, so you must love one another. By this everyone will know that you are my disciples, if you love one another.'
JOHN 13:31–35

E. Betrayal and trials

1. The betrayal and arrest of Jesus

Then he returned to the disciples and said to them, 'Are you still sleeping and resting? Look, the hour is near, and the Son of Man is betrayed into the hands of sinners. Rise, let us go! Here comes my betrayer!'

While he was still speaking, Judas, one of the Twelve, arrived. With him was a large crowd armed with swords and clubs, sent from the chief priests and the elders of the people. Now the betrayer had arranged a signal with them: 'The one I kiss is the man; arrest him.' Going at once to Jesus, Judas said, 'Greetings, Rabbi!' and kissed him.   MATTHEW 26:45–49

'Judas, are you betraying the Son of Man with a kiss?'   LUKE 22:48

Jesus replied, 'Friend, do what you came for.'

Then the men stepped forward, seized Jesus and arrested him. With that, one of Jesus' companions reached for his sword, drew it out and struck the servant of the high priest, cutting off his ear.

'Put your sword back in its place,' Jesus said to him, 'for all who draw the sword will die by the sword. Do you think I cannot call on my Father, and he will at once put at my disposal more than twelve legions of angels? But how then would the Scriptures be fulfilled that say it must happen in this way?'

At that time Jesus said to the crowd, 'Am I leading a rebellion, that you have come out with swords and clubs to capture me? Every day I sat in the temple courts teaching, and you did not arrest me. But this has all taken place that the writings of the prophets might be fulfilled.' Then all the disciples deserted him and fled.   MATTHEW 26:50–56

2. Jesus before Caiaphas

Meanwhile, the high priest questioned Jesus about his disciples and his teaching.

'I have spoken openly to the world,' Jesus replied. 'I always taught in synagogues or at the temple, where all the Jews come together. I said nothing in secret. Why question me? Ask those who heard me. Surely they know what I said.'

When Jesus said this, one of the officials near by struck him in the face. 'Is this the way you answer the high priest?' he demanded.

'If I said something wrong,' Jesus replied, 'testify as to what is wrong. But if I spoke the truth, why did you strike me?' Then Annas sent him, still bound, to Caiaphas the high priest.   JOHN
18:19–24

3. Jesus before Pilate

Pilate then went back inside the palace, summoned Jesus and asked him, 'Are you the king of the Jews?'

'Is that your own idea,' Jesus asked, 'or did others talk to you about me?'

'Am I a Jew?' Pilate replied. 'It was your people and your chief priests who handed you over to me. What is it you have done?'

Jesus said, 'My kingdom is not of this world. If it were, my servants would fight to prevent my arrest by the Jews. But now my kingdom is from another place.'

'You are a king, then!' said Pilate.

Jesus answered, 'You are right in saying I am a king. In fact, for this reason I was born, and for this I came into the world, to testify to the truth. Everyone on the side of truth listens to me.'   JOHN 18:33–37

4. Jesus speaks to the women of Jerusalem

As they led him away, they seized Simon from Cyrene, who was on his way in from the country, and put the cross on him and made him carry it behind Jesus. A large number of people followed him, including women who mourned and wailed for him. Jesus turned and said to them, 'Daughters of Jerusalem, do not weep for me; weep for yourselves and for your children. For the time will come when you will say, "Blessed are the barren women, the wombs that never bore and the breasts that never nursed!" Then

'"they will say to the mountains, 'Fall on us!'
    and to the hills 'Cover us!'"

For if people do these things when the tree is green, what will happen when it is dry?   LUKE 23:26–31

F. On the cross

1. Seven 'words' from the cross

'Father, forgive them'
'Father, forgive them, for they do not know what they are doing.'   LUKE 23:34

'Today you will be with me in paradise'
Jesus answered him [one of the criminals], 'I tell you the truth, today you will be with me in paradise.'   LUKE 23:43

'Here is your son.' 'Here is your mother.'
When Jesus saw his mother there, and the disciple whom he loved standing near by, he said to his mother, 'Dear woman, here is your son,' and to the disciple, 'Here is your mother.' From that time on, this disciple took her into his home.   JOHN 19:26–27

'I am thirsty'

Later, knowing that all was now completed, and so that the Scripture would be fulfilled, Jesus said, 'I am thirsty.' A jar of wine vinegar was there, so they soaked a sponge in it, put the sponge on a stalk of the hyssop plant, and lifted it to Jesus' lips.   JOHN 19:28–29

'Why have you forsaken me?'

From the sixth hour until the ninth hour darkness came over all the land. About the ninth hour Jesus cried out in a loud voice, *'Eloi, Eloi, lama sabachthani?'* – which means, 'My God, my God, why have you forsaken me?'   MATTHEW 27:45–46

'Father, into your hands I commit my spirit'

Jesus called out with a loud voice, 'Father, into your hands I commit my spirit.'   LUKE 23:46

'It is finished'

Jesus said: 'It is finished.' With that he bowed his head and gave up his life.   JOHN 19:30

G. Resurrection appearances

1. 'Do not be afraid'

After the Sabbath, at dawn on the first day of the week, Mary Magdalene and the other Mary went to look at the tomb . . .

So the women hurried away from the tomb, afraid yet filled with joy, and ran to tell his disciples. Suddenly Jesus met them. 'Greetings,' he said. They came to him, clasped his feet and worshipped him. Then Jesus said to them, 'Do not be afraid. Go and tell my brothers to go to Galilee; there they will see me.'   MATTHEW 28:1, 8–10

2. Jesus appears to Mary Magdalene

'Woman,' he said, 'why are you crying? Who is it you are looking for?'

Thinking he was the gardener, she said, 'Sir, if you have carried him away, tell me where you have put him, and I will get him.'

Jesus said to her, 'Mary.'

She turned towards him and cried out in Aramaic, 'Rabboni!' (which means Teacher).

Jesus said, 'Do not hold on to me, for I have not yet returned to the Father. Go instead to my brothers and tell them, "I am returning to my Father and your Father, to my God and your God."'

Mary Magdalene went to the disciples with the news: 'I have seen the Lord!' And she told them that he had said these things to her.   JOHN 20:15–18

3. Jesus broke bread and they recognised him

Now that same day two of them were going to a village called Emmaus, about seven miles from Jerusalem. They were talking with each other about everything that had happened. As they talked and discussed these things with each other, Jesus himself came up and walked along with them; but they were kept from recognising him.

He asked them, 'What are you discussing together as you walk along?'

They stood still, their faces downcast. One of them, named Cleopas, asked him, 'Are you only a visitor to Jerusalem and do not know the things that have happened there in these days?'

'What things?' he asked.

'About Jesus of Nazareth,' they replied. 'He was a prophet, powerful in word and deed before God and all the people. The chief priests and our rulers handed him over to be sentenced to death, and they crucified him; but we had hoped that he was the one who was going to redeem Israel. And what is more, it is the third day since all this took place. In addition, some of our women amazed us. They went to the tomb early this morning but didn't find his body. They came and told us that they had seen a vision of angels, who said he was alive. Then some of our companions went to the tomb and found it just as the women had said, but him they did not see.'

He said to them, 'How foolish you are, and how slow of heart to believe all that the prophets have spoken! Did not the Christ have to suffer these things and then enter his glory? And beginning with Moses and all the Prophets, he explained to them what was said in all the Scriptures concerning himself.

As they approached the village to which they were going, Jesus acted as if he were going further. But they urged him strongly, 'Stay with us, for it is nearly evening; the day is almost over.' So he went in to stay with them.

When he was at the table with them, he took bread, gave thanks, broke it and began to give it to them. Then their eyes were opened and they recognised him, and he disappeared from their sight. They asked each other, 'Were not our hearts burning within us while he talked with us on the road and opened the Scriptures to us?'

They got up and returned at once to Jerusalem. There they found the Eleven and those with them, assembled together and saying, 'It is true! The Lord has risen and has appeared to Simon.' Then the two told what had happened on the way, and how Jesus was recognised by them when he broke the bread.

LUKE 24:13–35

4. Jesus appears to his eleven disciples

While they were still talking about this, Jesus himself stood among them and said to them, "Peace be with you."

They were startled and frightened, thinking they saw a ghost. He said to them, 'Why are you troubled, and why do doubts rise in your minds? Look at my hands and my feet. It is I myself! Touch me and see; a ghost does not have flesh and bones, as you see I have.'

When he had said this, he showed them his hands and feet. And while they still did not believe it because of joy and amazement, he asked them, 'Do you have anything here to eat?' They gave him a piece of broiled fish, and he took it and ate it in their presence.   LUKE 24:36–43

5. 'You are witnesses of these things'

He said to them, 'This is what I told you while I was still with you: Everything must be fulfilled that is written about me in the Law of Moses, the Prophets and the Psalms.'

Then he opened their minds so they could understand the Scriptures. He told them, 'This is what is written: The Christ will suffer and rise from the dead on the third day, and repentance and forgiveness of sins will be preached in his name to all nations, beginning at Jerusalem. You are witnesses of these things. I am going to send you what my Father has promised; but stay in the city until you have been clothed with power from on high.'   LUKE 24:44–49

6. Jesus appears to Thomas

A week later his disciples were in the house again, and Thomas was with them. Though the doors were locked, Jesus came and stood among them and said, 'Peace be with you!' Then he said to Thomas, 'Put your finger here; see my hands. Reach out your hand and put it into my side. Stop doubting and believe.'

Thomas said to him, 'My Lord and my God!'

Then Jesus told him, 'Because you have seen me, you have believed; blessed are those who have not seen and yet have believed.'   JOHN 20:26–29

H. Ascension

In my former book, Theophilus, I wrote about all that Jesus began to do and to teach until the day he was taken up to heaven, after giving instructions through the Holy Spirit to the apostles he had chosen. After his suffering, he showed himself to them and gave many convincing proofs that he was alive. He appeared to them over a period of forty days and spoke about the kingdom of God. On one occasion, while he was eating with them, he gave them this command: 'Do not leave Jerusalem, but wait for the gift my Father promised, which you have heard me speak about. For John baptised with water, but in a few days you will be baptised with the Holy Spirit.'

So when they met together, they asked him, 'Lord, are you at this time going to restore the kingdom to Israel?'

He said to them: 'It is not for you to know the times or dates the Father has set by his own authority. But you will receive power when the Holy Spirit comes on you; and you will be my witnesses in Jerusalem, and in all Judea and Samaria, and to the ends of the earth.'

After he said this, he was taken up before their very eyes, and a cloud hid him from their sight.

They were looking intently up into the sky as he was going, when suddenly two men dressed in white stood beside them. 'You Galileans,' they said, 'why do you stand here looking into the sky? This same Jesus, who has been taken from you into heaven, will come back in the same way you have seen him go into heaven.'   ACTS 1:4–11

All the miracles of Jesus

	MATTHEW	MARK	LUKE	JOHN
PEOPLE HEALED				
A man with leprosy	8:1–4	1:40–42	5:12–13	
The centurion's servant	8:5–13		7:1–10	
Peter's mother-in-law	8:14–15	1:30–31	4:38–39	
Two men from Gadara	8:28–34	5:1–15	8:26–39	
A paralytic	9:2–7	2:3–12	5:17–26	
A woman with an incurable illness	9:20–22	5:25–29	8:43–48	
Two blind men	9:27–31			
A mute, demon-possessed man	9:32–34			
Man with shrivelled hand	12:10–13	3:1–5	6:6–10	
Man blind, mute and possessed	12:22			
Canaanite woman's daughter	15:21–28	7:24–30		
Boy with a demon	17:14–18	9:17–29	9:38–43	
Bartimaeus and another blind man	20:29–34	10:46–52	18:35–43	
A man possessed by an evil spirit		1:23–27	4:33–35	
A deaf and mute man		7:31–37		
A blind man at Bethsaida		8:22–26		
A woman bent double			13:10–17	
Man with dropsy			14:1–4	
Ten lepers			17:11–19	

All the miracles of Jesus

	MATTHEW	MARK	LUKE	JOHN
High priest's servant			22:50–51	
Official's son				4:46–54
An invalid at Bethesda				5:1–17
A man born blind				9:1–7; 35–41

PEOPLE BROUGHT BACK TO LIFE

	MATTHEW	MARK	LUKE	JOHN
A dead girl	9:18–19, 23–25	5:22–24, 38–42	8:40–42, 49–56	
A widow's son			7:11–15	
Lazarus				11:1–44

NATURE MIRACLES

	MATTHEW	MARK	LUKE	JOHN
Calming a storm	8:23–27	4:35–41	8:22–25	
5,000 people fed	14:13–21	6:35–44	9:12–17	6:5–13
Jesus walks on the water	14:22–33	6:48–51		6:19–21
4,000 people fed	15:32–38	8:1–9		
Coin in a fish's mouth	17:24–27			
Fig-tree withered	21:18–22	11:12–14, 20–25		
Catch of fish			5:1–11	21:1–11
Water changed into wine				2:1–11
A catch of 153 fish				21:1–11

❧ THE HEALINGS OF JESUS ❧

A. Demon-possessed people

1. Many demon-possessed people

When evening came, many who were demon-possessed were brought to him, and he drove out the spirits with a word and healed all the sick. This was to fulfil what was spoken through the prophet Isaiah:

> 'He took up our infirmities
> and carried our diseases.' MATTHEW 8:16–17

2. A man possessed by an evil spirit

Just then a man in their synagogue who was possessed by an evil spirit cried out, 'What do you want with us, Jesus of Nazareth? Have you come to destroy us? I know who you are – the Holy One of God!'

'Be quiet!' said Jesus sternly. 'Come out of him!' The evil spirit shook the man violently and came out of him with a shriek.

The people were all so amazed that they asked each other, 'What is this? A new teaching – and with authority! He even gives orders to evil spirits and they obey him.' MARK 1:23–27

3. A man nicknamed Legion

They sailed to the region of the Gerasenes, which is across the lake from Galilee. When Jesus stepped ashore, he was met by a demon-possessed man from the town. For a long time this man had not worn clothes or lived in a house, but had lived in the tombs. When he saw Jesus, he cried out and fell at his feet, shouting at the top of his voice, 'What do you want with me, Jesus, Son of the Most High God? I beg you, don't torture me!'

For Jesus had commanded the evil spirit to come out of the man. Many times it had seized him, and though he was chained hand and foot and kept under guard, he had broken his chains and had been driven by the demon into solitary places.

Jesus asked him, 'What is your name?'

'Legion,' he replied, because many demons had gone into him. And they begged him repeatedly not to order them to go into the Abyss.

A large herd of pigs was feeding there on the hillside. The demons begged Jesus to let them go into them, and he gave them permission. When the demons came out of the man, they went into the pigs, and the herd rushed down the steep bank into the lake and was drowned.

When those tending the pigs saw what had happened, they ran off and reported this in the town and countryside, and the people went out to see what had happened. When they came to Jesus, they found the man from whom the demons had gone out, sitting at Jesus' feet, dressed and in his right mind; and they were afraid. Those who had seen it told the people how the demon-possessed man had been cured. Then all the people of the region of the Gerasenes asked Jesus to leave them, because they were overcome with fear. So he got into the boat and left.

The man from whom the demons had gone out begged to go with him, but Jesus sent him away, saying, 'Return home and tell how much God has done for you.' So the man went away and told all over the town how much Jesus had done for him.   LUKE 8:26–39

4. A mute, demon-possessed man

While they were going out, a man who was demon-possessed and could not talk was brought to Jesus. And when the demon was driven out, the man who had been dumb spoke. The crowd was amazed and said, 'Nothing like this has ever been seen in Israel.'

But the Pharisees said, 'It is by the prince of demons that he drives out demons.'   MATTHEW 9:32–34

B. Deaf, mute, blind and paralysed people

1. A man born blind

'Go, wash in the pool of Siloam'

As he went along, he saw a man blind from birth. His disciples asked him, 'Rabbi, who sinned, this man or his parents, that he was born blind?'

'Neither this man nor his parents sinned,' said Jesus, 'but this happened so that the work of God might be displayed in his life. As long as it is day, we must do the work of him who sent me. Night is coming, when no-one can work. While I am in the world, I am the light of the world.'

Having said this, he spat on the ground, made some mud with the saliva, and put it on the man's eyes. 'Go,' he told him, 'wash in the pool of Siloam' (this word means Sent). So the man went and washed, and came home seeing.

Spiritual blindness

Jesus heard that they [the Pharisees] had thrown him out [of the synagogue], and when he found him, he said, 'Do you believe in the Son of Man?'

'Who is he, sir?' the man asked. 'Tell me so that I may believe in him.'

Jesus said, 'You have now seen him; in fact, he is the one speaking with you.'

Then the man said, 'Lord, I believe,' and he worshipped him.

Jesus said, 'For judgment I have come into this world, so that the blind will see and those who see will become blind.'

Some Pharisees who were with him heard him say this and asked, 'What? Are we blind too?'

Jesus said, 'If you were blind, you would not be guilty of sin; but now that you claim you can see, your guilt remains.'   JOHN 9:1–7; 35–41

2. Two blind men

As Jesus went on from there, two blind men followed him, calling out, 'Have mercy on us, Son of David!'

When he had gone indoors, the blind men came to him, and he asked them, 'Do you believe that I am able to do this?'

'Yes, Lord,' they replied.

Then he touched their eyes and said, 'According to your faith will it be done to you'; and their sight was restored. Jesus warned them sternly, 'See that no-one knows about this.' But they went out and spread the news about him all over that region.   MATTHEW 9:27–31

3. Two more blind men

As Jesus and his disciples were leaving Jericho, a large crowd followed him. Two blind men were sitting by the roadside, and when they heard that Jesus was going by, they shouted, 'Lord, Son of David, have mercy on us!'

The crowd rebuked them and told them to be quiet, but they shouted all the louder. 'Lord, Son of David, have mercy on us!'

Jesus stopped and called them. 'What do you want me to do for you?' he asked.

'Lord,' they answered, 'we want our sight.'

Jesus had compassion on them and touched their eyes. Immediately they received their sight and followed him.
MATTHEW 20:29–34

4. Bartimaeus, the blind beggar

Then they came to Jericho. As Jesus and his disciples, together with a large crowd, were leaving the city, a blind man, Bartimaeus (that is, the Son of Timaeus), was sitting by the roadside begging. When he heard that it was Jesus of Nazareth, he began to shout,'Jesus, Son of David, have mercy on me!'

Many rebuked him and told him to be quiet, but he shouted all the more, 'Son of David, have mercy on me!'

Jesus stopped and said, 'Call him.'

So they called to the blind man, 'Cheer up! On your feet! He's calling you.' Throwing his cloak aside, he jumped to his feet and came to Jesus.

'What do you want me to do for you?' Jesus asked him.

The blind man said, 'Rabbi, I want to see.'

'Go,' said Jesus, 'your faith has healed you.' Immediately he received his sight and followed Jesus along the road.   MARK 10:46–52

5. 'Ephphatha!' 'Be opened!'

Then Jesus left the vicinity of Tyre and went through Sidon, down to the Sea of Galilee and into the region of the Decapolis. There some people brought a man to him who was deaf and could hardly talk, and they begged him to place his hand on him.

After he took him aside, away from the crowd, Jesus put his fingers into the man's ears. Then he spat and touched the man's tongue. He looked up to heaven and with a deep sigh said to him, 'Ephphatha!' (which means, 'Be opened!'). At this, the man's ears were opened, his tongue was loosened and he began to speak plainly.

Jesus commanded them not to tell anyone. But the more he did so, the more they kept talking about it. People were over- whelmed with amazement. 'He has done everything well,' they said. 'He even makes the deaf hear and the mute speak.'   MARK 7:31–37

6. A blind man at Bethsaida

They came to Bethsaida, and some people brought a blind man and begged Jesus to touch him. He took the blind man by the hand and led him outside the village. When he had spat on the man's eyes and put his hands on him, Jesus asked, 'Do you see anything?'

He looked up and said, 'I see people; they look like trees walking around.'

Once more Jesus put his hands on the man's eyes. Then his eyes were opened, his sight was restored, and he saw everything clearly. Jesus sent him home, saying, 'Don't go into the village.' MARK 8:22–26

7. A paralytic

One day as he was teaching, Pharisees and teachers of the law, who had come from every village of Galilee and from Judea and Jerusalem, were sitting there. And the power of the Lord was present for him to heal the sick. Some people came carrying a paralytic on a mat and tried to take him into the house to lay him before Jesus. When they could not find a way to do this because of the crowd, they went up on the roof and lowered him on his mat through the tiles into the middle of the crowd, right in front of Jesus.

When Jesus saw their faith, he said, 'Friend, your sins are forgiven.'

The Pharisees and the teachers of the law began thinking to themselves, 'Who is this fellow who speaks blasphemy? Who can forgive sins but God alone?'

Jesus knew what they were thinking and asked, 'Why are you thinking these things in your hearts? Which is easier: to say, "Your sins are forgiven," or to say, "Get up and walk"? But that you may know that the Son of Man has authority on earth to forgive sins . . .' He said to the paralysed man, 'I tell you, get up, take your mat and go home.' Immediately he stood up in front of them, took what he had been lying on and went home praising God. Everyone was amazed and gave praise to God. They were filled with awe and said, 'We have seen remarkable things today.' LUKE 5:17–26

C. People healed at a distance from Jesus

1. The centurion's servant

When Jesus had entered Capernaum, a centurion came to him, asking for help. 'Lord,' he said, 'my servant lies at home paralysed and in terrible suffering.'

Jesus said to him, 'I will go and heal him.'

The centurion replied, 'Lord, I do not deserve to have you come under my roof. But just say the word, and my servant will be healed. For I myself am a man under authority, with soldiers under me. I tell this one, "Go," and he goes; and that one, "Come," and he comes. I say to my servant, "Do this," and he does it.'

When Jesus heard this, he was astonished and said to those following him, 'I tell you the truth, I have not found anyone in Israel with such great faith. I say to you that many will come from the east and the west, and will take their places at the feast with Abraham, Isaac and Jacob in the kingdom of heaven. But the subjects of the kingdom will be thrown outside, into the darkness, where there will be weeping and gnashing of teeth.'

Then Jesus said to the centurion, 'Go! It will be done just as you believed it would.' And his servant was healed at that very hour.   MATTHEW 8:5–13

2. A royal official's son

Once more he visited Cana in Galilee, where he had turned the water into wine. And there was a certain royal official whose son lay sick at Capernaum. When this man heard that Jesus had arrived in Galilee from Judea, he went to him and begged him to come and heal his son, who was close to death.

'Unless you people see miraculous signs and wonders,' Jesus told him, 'you will never believe.'

The royal official said, 'Sir, come down before my child dies.'

Jesus replied, 'You may go. Your son will live.'

The man took Jesus at his word and departed. While he was still on the way, his servants met him with the news that his boy was living. When he enquired as to the time when his son got better, they said to him, 'The fever left him yesterday at the seventh hour.'

Then the father realised that this was the exact time at which Jesus had said to him, 'Your son will live.' So he and all his household believed.

This was the second miraculous sign that Jesus performed, having come from Judea to Galilee.   JOHN 4:46–54

D. People with leprosy and fevers

1. A man with leprosy

When he came down from the mountainside, large crowds followed him. A man with leprosy came and knelt before him and said, 'Lord, if you are willing, you can make me clean.'

Jesus reached out his hand and touched the man. 'I am willing,' he said. 'Be clean!' Immediately he was cured of his leprosy. Then Jesus said to him, 'See that you don't tell anyone. But go, show yourself to the priest and offer the gift Moses commanded, as a testimony to them.'   MATTHEW 8:1–4

2. Ten lepers

Now on his way to Jerusalem, Jesus travelled along the border between Samaria and Galilee. As he was going into a village, ten men who had leprosy met him. They stood at a distance and called out in a loud voice, 'Jesus, Master, have pity on us!'

When he saw them, he said, 'Go, show yourselves to the priests.' And as they went, they were cleansed.

One of them, when he saw he was healed, came back, praising God in a loud voice. He threw himself at Jesus' feet and thanked him – and he was a Samaritan.

Jesus asked, 'Were not all ten cleansed? Where are the other nine? Was no-one found to return and give praise to God except this foreigner?' Then he said to him, 'Rise and go; your faith has made you well.'   LUKE 17:11–19

3. The fever of Peter's mother-in-law

When Jesus came into Peter's house, he saw Peter's mother-in-law lying in bed with a fever. He touched her hand and the fever left her, and she got up and began to wait on him.   MATTHEW 8:14–15

E. People with long-term illnesses

1. A woman bent double for eighteen years

On a Sabbath Jesus was teaching in one of the synagogues, and a woman was there who had been crippled by a spirit for eighteen years. She was bent over and could not straighten up at all. When Jesus saw her, he called her forward and said to her, 'Woman, you are set free from your infirmity.' Then he put his hands on her, and immediately she straightened up and praised God.

Indignant because Jesus had healed on the Sabbath, the synagogue ruler said to the people, 'There are six days for work. So come and be healed on those days, not on the Sabbath.'

The Lord answered him, 'You hypocrites! Doesn't each of you on the Sabbath untie his ox or donkey from the stall and lead it out to give it water? Then should not this woman, a daughter of Abraham whom Satan has kept bound for eighteen long years, be set free on the Sabbath day from what bound her?'   LUKE 13:10–17

2. '. . . An invalid for thirty-eight years'

Some time later, Jesus went up to Jerusalem for a feast of the Jews. Now there is in Jerusalem near the Sheep Gate a pool, which in Aramaic is called Bethesda and which is surrounded by five covered colonnades. Here a great number of disabled people used to lie – the blind, the lame, the paralysed. One who was there had been an invalid for thirty-eight years. When Jesus saw him lying there and learned that he had been in this condition for a long time, he asked him, 'Do you want to get well?'

'Sir,' the invalid replied, 'I have no-one to help me into the pool when the water is stirred. While I am trying to get in, someone else goes down ahead of me.'

Then Jesus said to him, 'Get up! Pick up your mat and walk.' At once the man was cured; he picked up his mat and walked.

The day on which this took place was a Sabbath, and so the Jews said to the man who had been healed, 'It is the Sabbath; the law forbids you to carry your mat.'

But he replied, 'The man who made me well said to me, "Pick up your mat and walk."'

So they asked him, 'Who is this fellow who told you to pick it up and walk?'

The man who was healed had no idea who it was, for Jesus had slipped away into the crowd that was there.

Later Jesus found him at the temple and said to him, 'See, you are well again. Stop sinning or something worse may happen to you.' The man went away and told the Jews that it was Jesus who had made him well.

So, because Jesus was doing these things on the Sabbath, the Jews persecuted him. Jesus said to them, 'My Father is always at his work to this very day, and I, too, am working.' JOHN 5:1–17

3. A woman who had an incurable illness

As Jesus was on his way, the crowds almost crushed him. And a woman was there who had been subject to bleeding for twelve years, but no-one could heal her. She came up behind him and touched the edge of his cloak, and immediately her bleeding stopped.

'Who touched me?' Jesus asked.

When they all denied it, Peter said, 'Master, the people are crowding and pressing against you.'

But Jesus said, 'Someone touched me; I know that power has gone out from me.'

Then the woman, seeing that she could not go unnoticed, came trembling and fell at his feet. In the presence of all the people, she told why she had touched him and how she had been instantly healed. Then he said to her, 'Daughter, your faith has healed you. Go in peace.'   LUKE 8:42b–48

F. Dead people

1. An only daughter

Now when Jesus returned, a crowd welcomed him, for they were all expecting him. Then a man named Jairus, a ruler of the synagogue, came and fell at Jesus' feet, pleading with him to come to his house because his only daughter, a girl of about twelve, was dying . . .

While Jesus was still speaking, someone came from the house of Jairus, the synagogue ruler. 'Your daughter is dead,' he said. 'Don't bother the teacher any more.'

Hearing this, Jesus said to Jairus, 'Don't be afraid; just believe, and she will be healed.'

When he arrived at the house of Jairus, he did not let anyone go in with him except Peter, John and James, and the child's father and mother. Meanwhile, all the people were wailing and mourning for her. 'Stop wailing,' Jesus said. 'She is not dead but asleep.'

They laughed at him, knowing that she was dead. But he took

her by the hand and said, 'My child, get up!' Her spirit returned, and at once she stood up. Then Jesus told them to give her something to eat. Her parents were astonished, but he ordered them not to tell anyone what had happened.   LUKE 8:40–42a; 49–56

2. A widow's son

Soon afterwards, Jesus went to a town called Nain, and his disciples and a large crowd went along with him. As he approached the town gate, a dead person was being carried out – the only son of his mother, and she was a widow. And a large crowd from the town was with her. When the Lord asaw her, his heart went out to her and he said, 'Don't cry.'

Then he went up and touched the coffin, and those carrying it stood still. He said, 'Young man, I say to you, get up!' The dead man sat up and began to talk, and Jesus gave him back to his mother.   LUKE 7:11–15

❧ THE MIRACLES OF JESUS ☙

1. Calming a storm

That day when evening came, he said to his disciples, 'Let us go over to the other side.' Leaving the crowd behind, they took him along, just as he was, in the boat. There were also other boats with him. A furious squall came up, and the waves broke over the boat, so that it was nearly swamped. Jesus was in the stern, sleeping on a cushion. The disciples woke him and said to him, 'Teacher, don't you care if we drown?'

He got up, rebuked the wind and said to the waves, 'Quiet! Be still!' Then the wind died down and it was completely calm.

He said to his disciples, 'Why are you so afraid? Do you still have no faith?'

They were terrified and asked each other, 'Who is this? Even the wind and the waves obey him!'   MARK 4:35–41

2. Jesus walks on the water

Immediately Jesus made the disciples get into the boat and go on ahead of him to the other side, while he dismissed the crowd. After he had dismissed them, he went up on a mountainside by himself to pray. When evening came, he was there alone, but the boat was already a considerable distance from land, buffeted by the waves because the wind was against it.

During the fourth watch of the night Jesus went out to them, walking on the lake. When the disciples saw him walking on the lake, they were terrified. 'It's a ghost,' they said, and cried out in fear.

But Jesus immediately said to them: 'Take courage! It is I. Don't be afraid.'

'Lord, if it's you,' Peter replied, 'Tell me to come to you on the water.'

'Come,' he said.

Then Peter got down out of the boat, walked on the water and came towards Jesus. But when he saw the wind, he was afraid and, beginning to sink, cried out, 'Lord, save me!'

Immediately Jesus reached out his hand and caught him. 'You of little faith,' he said, 'why did you doubt?'

And when they climbed into the boat, the wind died down. Then those who were in the boat worshipped him, saying, 'Truly you are the Son of God.'   MATTHEW 14:22–33

3. Water changed into wine

On the third day a wedding took place at Cana in Galilee. Jesus' mother was there, and Jesus and his disciples had also been invited to the wedding. When the wine was gone, Jesus' mother said to him, 'They have no more wine.'

'Dear woman, why do you involve me?' Jesus replied, 'My time has not yet come.'

His mother said to the servants, 'Do whatever he tells you.'

Nearby stood six stone water jars, the kind used by the Jews for ceremonial washing, each holding from twenty to thirty gallons.

Jesus said to the servants, 'Fill the jars with water'; so they filled them to the brim.

Then he told them, 'Now draw some out and take it to the master of the banquet.'

They did so, and the master of the banquet tasted the water that had been turned into wine. He did not realise where it had come from, though the servants who had drawn the water knew. Then he called the bridegroom aside and said, 'Everyone brings out the choice wine first and then the cheaper wine after the guests have had too much to drink; but you have saved the best till now.'

This, the first of his miraculous signs, Jesus performed at Cana in Galilee. He thus revealed his glory, and his disciples put their faith in him.   JOHN 2:1–11

4. A catch of 153 fish

That night they caught nothing

Afterwards Jesus appeared again to his disciples by the Sea of Tiberias. It happened this way: Simon Peter, Thomas (called Didymus), Nathanael from Cana in Galilee, the sons of Zebedee, and two other disciples were together. 'I'm going out to fish,' Simon Peter told them, and they said, 'We'll go with you.' So they went out and got into the boat, but that night they caught nothing.

Early in the morning, Jesus stood on the shore, but the disciples did not realise that it was Jesus.

He called out to them, 'Friends, haven't you any fish?'

'No,' they answered.

'It is the Lord!'

He said, 'Throw your net on the right side of the boat and you will find some.' When they did, they were unable to haul the net in because of the large number of fish.

Then the disciple whom Jesus loved said to Peter, 'It is the Lord!' As soon as Simon Peter heard him say 'It is the Lord,' he wrapped his outer garment around him (for he had taken it off) and jumped into the water. The other disciples followed in the boat, towing the net full of fish, for they were not far from shore, about a hundred yards. When they landed, they saw a fire of burning coals there with fish on it, and some bread.

'Come and have breakfast'
Jesus said to them, 'Bring some of the fish you have just caught.'

Simon Peter climbed aboard and dragged the net ashore. It was full of large fish, 153, but even with so many the net was not torn.   JOHN 21:1–11

5. Five thousand people fed

When Jesus heard what had happened, he withdrew by boat privately to a solitary place. Hearing of this, the crowds followed him on foot from the towns. When Jesus landed and saw a large crowd, he had compassion on them and healed their sick.

As evening approached, the disciples came to him and said, 'This is a remote place, and it's already getting late. Send the crowds away, so that they can go to the villages and buy themselves some food.'

Jesus replied, 'They do not need to go away. You give them something to eat.'

'We have here only five loaves of bread and two fish,' they answered.

'Bring them here to me,' he said. And he directed the people to sit down on the grass. Taking the five loaves and the two fish and looking up to heaven, he gave thanks and broke the loaves. Then he gave them to the disciples, and the disciples gave them to the people. They all ate and were satisfied, and the disciples picked up twelve basketfuls of broken pieces that were left over. The number of those who ate was about five thousand men, besides women and children.   MATTHEW 14:13–21

6. Four thousand people fed

Jesus called his disciples to him and said, 'I have compassion for these people; they have already been with me three days and have nothing to eat. I do not want to send them away hungry, or they may collapse on the way.'

His disciples answered, 'Where could we get enough bread in this remote place to feed such a crowd?'

'How many loaves do you have?' Jesus asked.

'Seven,' they replied, 'and a few small fish.'

He told the crowd to sit down on the ground. Then he took the seven loaves and the fish, and when he had given thanks, he broke them and gave them to the disciples, and they in turn to the people. They all ate and were satisfied. Afterwards the disciples picked up seven basketfuls of broken pieces that were left over. The number of those who ate was four thousand men, besides women and children.   MATTHEW 15:32–38

7. Cities where most miracles took place

Then Jesus began to denounce the cities in which most of his miracles had been performed, because they did not repent. 'Woe to you, Korazin! Woe to you, Bethsaida! If the miracles that were performed in you had been performed in Tyre and Sidon, they would have repented long ago in sackcloth and ashes. But I tell you, it will be more bearable for Tyre and Sidon on the day of judgment than for you. And you, Capernaum, will you be lifted up to the skies? No, you will go down to the depths. If the miracles that were performed in you had been performed in Sodom, it would have remained to this day. But I tell you that it will be more bearable for Sodom on the day of judgment than for you.'   MATTHEW 11:20–24

PART 3

WHAT JESUS PRAYED

✎ WHERE JESUS PRAYED ✎

1. On a mountainside

Jesus made his disciples get into the boat and go on ahead of him to Bethsaida, while he dismissed the crowd. After leaving them, he went up on a mountainside to pray.   MARK 6:45–46

2. In a garden

Jesus went out as usual to the Mount of Olives, and his disciples followed him. On reaching the place, he said to them, 'Pray . . .'   LUKE 22:39–40

3. In synagogues

He [Jesus] went to Nazareth, where he had been brought up, and on the Sabbath day he went into the synagogue, as was his custom.   LUKE 4:16

4. From the cross

When the came to the place called the Skull, there they crucified him . . . Jesus said, 'Father, forgive them, for they do not know what they are doing.'   LUKE 23:33–34

✎ *WHEN JESUS PRAYED* ✎

1. Before he chose the twelve apostles

Jesus went out to a mountainside to pray, and spent the night praying to God. When morning came, he called his disciples to him and chose twelve of them, whom he also designated apostles.   LUKE 6:12–13

2. Before his transfiguration

Jesus . . . took Peter, John and James with him and went up onto a mountain to pray. As he was praying, the appearance of his face changed.   LUKE 9:28–29

3. Facing his biggest crisis

Then Jesus went with his disciples to a place called Gethsemane, and he said to them, 'Sit here while I go over there and pray.' He took Peter and the two sons of Zebedee along with him, and he began to be sorrowful and troubled. Then he said to them, 'My soul is overwhelmed with sorrow to the point of death. Stay here and keep watch with me.'

Going a little farther, he fell with his face to the ground and prayed. 'My Father, if it is possible, may this cup be taken from me. Yet not as I will, but as you will.'

Then he returned to his disciples and found them sleeping. 'Couldn't you keep watch with me for one hour?' he asked Peter. 'Watch and pray so that you will not fall into temptation. The spirit is willing, but the body is weak.'

He went away a second time and prayed, 'My Father, if it is not possible for this cup to be taken away unless I drink it, may your will be done.'

When he came back, he again found them sleeping, because

their eyes were heavy. So he left them and went away once more and prayed the third time, saying the same thing. MATTHEW 26:36–44

✵ *WHAT JESUS PRAYED* ✵

1. The Lord's Prayer

'This, then, is how you should pray:
  '"Our Father in heaven,
  hallowed be your name,
  your kingdom come,
  your will be done
    on earth as it is in heaven.
  Give us today our daily bread.
  Forgive us our debts,
    as we also have forgiven our debtors.
  And lead us not into temptation,
  but deliver us from the evil one."' MATTHEW 6:9–13

2. Jesus prays with joy

At that time Jesus, full of joy through the Holy Spirit, said, 'I praise you, Father, Lord of heaven and earth, because you have hidden these things from the wise and learned, and revealed them to little children. Yes, Father, for this was your good pleasure.

'All things have been committed to me by my Father. No-one knows who the Son is except the Father, and no-one knows who the Father is except the Son and those to whom the Son chooses to reveal him.' LUKE 10:21–22

3. Jesus prays for himself

After Jesus said this, he looked towards heaven and prayed:

'Father, the time has come. Glorify your Son, that your Son may glorify you. For you granted him authority over all people that he might give eternal life to all those you have given him. Now this is eternal life: that they may know you, the only true God, and Jesus Christ, whom you have sent. I have brought you glory on earth by completing the work you gave me to do. And now, Father, glorify me in your presence with the glory I had with you before the world began.' JOHN 17:1–5

4. Jesus prays for his followers

'Protect them by the power of your name'

'I have revealed you to those whom you gave me out of the world. They were yours; you gave them to me and they have obeyed your word. Now they know that everything you have given me comes from you. For I gave them the words you gave me and they accepted them. They knew with certainty that I came from you, and they believed that you sent me. I pray for them. I am not praying for the world, but for those you have given me, for they are yours. All I have is yours, and all you have is mine. And glory has come to me through them. I will remain in the world no longer, but they are still in the world, and I am coming to you. Holy Father, protect them by the power of your name – the name you gave me – so that they may be one as we are one. While I was with them, I protected them, and kept them safe by that name you gave me. None has been lost except the one doomed to destruction so that Scripture would be fulfilled.'

'Sanctify them by the truth'

'I am coming to you now, but I say these things while I am still in the world, so that they may have the full measure of my joy within them. I have given them your word and the world has hated them, for they are not of the world any more than I am of the world. My prayer is not that you take them out of the world but that you protect them from the evil one. They are not of the world, even as I am not of it. Sanctify them by the truth; your word is truth. As you sent me into the world, I have sent them into the world. For them I sanctify myself, that they too may be truly sanctified.'   JOHN 17:6–19

5. Jesus prays for future believers

'I pray that all of them may be one'

'My prayer is not for them alone. I pray also for those who will believe in me through their message, that all of them may be one, Father, just as you are in me and I am in you. May they also be in us so that the world may believe that you have sent me. I have given them the glory that you gave me, that they may be one as we are one: I in them and you in me. May they be brought to complete unity to let the world know that you sent me and have loved them even as you have loved me.'

'I want them to see my glory'

'Father, I want those you have given me to be with me where I am, and to see my glory, the glory you have given me because you loved me before the creation of the world.

'Righteous Father, though the world does not know you, I know you, and they know that you have sent me. I have made you known to them, and will continue to make you known in order that the love you have for me may be in them and that I myself may be in them.'   JOHN 17:20–26

❧ *TEACHING ABOUT PRAYER* ❧

1. The wise and foolish builders

'Why do you call me, "Lord, Lord," and do not do what I say? I will show you what people are like who come to me and hear my words and put them into practice. They are like a man building a house, who dug down deep and laid the foundation on rock. When the flood came, the torrent struck that house but could not shake it, because it was well built. But those who hear my words and do not put them into practice are like a man who built a house on the ground without a foundation. The moment the torrent struck that house, it collapsed and its destruction was complete.'   LUKE 6:46–49

2. 'The man's persistence'

Then he said to them, 'Suppose one of you has a friend, and he goes to him at midnight and says, "Friend, lend me three loaves of bread, because a friend of mine on a journey has come to me, and I have nothing to set before him."

'Then the one inside answers, "Don't bother me. The door is already locked, and my children are with me in bed. I can't get up and give you anything." I tell you, though he will not get up and give him the bread because he is his friend, yet because of the man's boldness he will get up and give him as much as he needs.'   LUKE 11:5–8

3. The widow and the judge

Then Jesus told his disciples a parable to show them that they should always pray and not give up. He said: 'In a certain town there was a judge who neither feared God nor cared about people. And there was a widow in that town who kept coming to him with the plea, "Grant me justice against my adversary."

'For some time he refused. But finally he said to himself, "Even though I don't fear God or care about people, yet because this widow keeps bothering me, I will see that she gets justice, so that she won't eventually wear me out with her coming!"'

And the Lord said, 'Listen to what the unjust judge says. And will not God bring about justice for his chosen ones, who cry out to him day and night? Will he keep putting them off? I tell you, he will see that they get justice, and quickly. However, when the Son of Man comes, will he find faith on the earth?' LUKE 18:1–8

4. 'Don't pray like the hypocrites'

'And when you pray, do not be like the hypocrites, for they love to pray standing in the synagogues and on the street corners to be seen by others. I tell you the truth, they have received their reward in full.' MATTHEW 6:5

5. Pray in secret

'But when you pray, go into your room, close the door and pray to your Father, who is unseen. Then your Father, who sees what is done in secret, will reward you.' MATTHEW 6:6

6. Don't pray meaningless prayers

'And when you pray, do not keep on babbling like pagans, for they think they will be heard because of their many words. Do not be like them, for your Father knows what you need before you ask him.' MATTHEW 6:7–8

7. *Forgiving and not forgiving others*

'For if you forgive others when they sin against you, your heavenly Father will also forgive you. But if you do not forgive others their sins, your Father will not forgive your sins.'
MATTHEW 6:14–15

8. *Ask, seek, knock*

'Ask and it will be given to you; seek and you will find; knock and the door will be opened to you. For everyone who asks receives; everyone who seeks finds; and to everyone who knocks, the door will be opened.

'Which of you, if your children ask for bread, will give them a stone? Or if they ask for a fish, will give them a snake? If you, then, though you are evil, know how to give good gifts to your children, how much more will your Father in heaven give good gifts to those who ask him!'   MATTHEW 7:7–11

9. *Ask and you will receive*

'In that day you will no longer ask me anything. I tell you the truth, my Father will give you whatever you ask in my name. Until now you have not asked for anything in my name. Ask and you will receive, and your joy will be complete.

'Though I have been speaking figuratively, a time is coming when I will no longer use this kind of language but will tell you plainly about my Father. In that day you will ask in my name. I am not saying that I will ask the Father on your behalf. No, the Father himself loves you because you have loved me and have believed that I came from God. I came from the Father and entered the world; now I am leaving the world and going back to the Father.'   JOHN 16:23–28

10. The gift of the Holy Spirit

'If you then, though you are evil, know how to give good gifts to your children, how much more will your Father in heaven give the Holy Spirit to those who ask him!' LUKE 11:13

11. Agreeing in prayer

'Again, I tell you that if two of you on earth agree about anything you ask for, it will be done for you by my Father in heaven.' MATTHEW 18:19

12. Jesus' presence during prayer

'For where two or three come together in my name, there am I with them.' MATTHEW 18:20

13. Pray for those who ill-treat you

'Bless those who curse you, pray for those who ill-treat you.' LUKE 6:28

14. 'Pray that you will not fall into temptation'

Jesus went out as usual to the Mount of Olives, and his disciples followed him. On reaching the place, he said to them, 'Pray that you will not fall into temptation.' LUKE 22:39–40

APPENDIX

FOUR PORTRAITS
OF JESUS

Here is a way of reading through
the four portraits of Jesus,
given by Matthew, Mark, Luke and John
– one chapter a day.

Reading through St Matthew's Gospel

Day	Tick Box	Chapter	
1	☐	Matt. 1	The birth of Jesus
2	☐	Matt. 2	The early years of Jesus
3	☐	Matt. 3	Jesus is baptised
4	☐	Matt. 4	Jesus starts his work
5	☐	Matt. 5	The Sermon on the Mount: part 1
6	☐	Matt. 6	The Sermon on the Mount: part 2
7	☐	Matt. 7	The Sermon on the Mount: part 3
8	☐	Matt. 8	Three healing miracles
9	☐	Matt. 9	Life, sight and speech are restored
10	☐	Matt. 10	The twelve apostles are taught
11	☐	Matt. 11	Jesus answers John the Baptist
12	☐	Matt. 12	The Pharisees object to Jesus
13	☐	Matt. 13	Parables about the kingdom
14	☐	Matt. 14	Jesus mourns for John the Baptist
15	☐	Matt. 15	Arguments and miracles
16	☐	Matt. 16	Peter says who Jesus is
17	☐	Matt. 17	The transfiguration of Jesus
18	☐	Matt. 18	Teaching about forgiveness
19	☐	Matt. 19	Teaching about wealth
20	☐	Matt. 20	The parable of the labourers
21	☐	Matt. 21	Jesus enters Jerusalem
22	☐	Matt. 22	People oppose Jesus
23	☐	Matt. 23	Jesus condemns the Pharisees
24	☐	Matt. 24	Jesus teaches about the future
25	☐	Matt. 25	Jesus teaches about judgment
26	☐	Matt. 26	The Last Supper
27	☐	Matt. 27	Jesus is crucified
28	☐	Matt. 28	The resurrection of Jesus

Reading through St Mark's Gospel

Day	Tick Box	Chapter	
1	☐	Mark 1	Jesus starts his work
2	☐	Mark 2	Religious people oppose Jesus
3	☐	Mark 3	Jesus appoints the twelve apostles
4	☐	Mark 4	Parables by the seaside
5	☐	Mark 5	Three miracles
6	☐	Mark 6	John the Baptist is martyred
7	☐	Mark 7	The Pharisees argue with Jesus
8	☐	Mark 8	Peter says who Jesus is
9	☐	Mark 9	Jesus is transfigured
10	☐	Mark 10	Jesus teaches about wealth
11	☐	Mark 11	Jesus enters Jerusalem
12	☐	Mark 12	Religious leaders oppose Jesus
13	☐	Mark 13	Jesus teaches about the future
14	☐	Mark 14	Judas betrays Jesus
15	☐	Mark 15	Jesus is crucified
16	☐	Mark 16	The resurrection of Jesus

Reading through St Luke's Gospel

Day	Tick Box	Chapter	
1	☐	Luke 1	John the Baptist is born
2	☐	Luke 2	Jesus is born
3	☐	Luke 3	John baptises Jesus
4	☐	Luke 4	Jesus starts his work
5	☐	Luke 5	Two healing miracles
6	☐	Luke 6	Jesus appoints the twelve apostles
7	☐	Luke 7	Jesus praises John the Baptist
8	☐	Luke 8	Two parables, and four miracles
9	☐	Luke 9	Jesus is transfigured
10	☐	Luke 10	Seventy more disciples
11	☐	Luke 11	Religious leaders reject Jesus
12	☐	Luke 12	Jesus gives five warnings
13	☐	Luke 13	Jesus teaches about the kingdom
14	☐	Luke 14	Jesus teaches about discipleship
15	☐	Luke 15	Three parables about being lost
16	☐	Luke 16	The rich man and Lazarus
17	☐	Luke 17	Jesus and the second coming
18	☐	Luke 18	Jesus teaches about prayer
19	☐	Luke 19	Jesus enters Jerusalem
20	☐	Luke 20	Religious leaders question Jesus
21	☐	Luke 21	The signs of the coming of Jesus
22	☐	Luke 22	The Passover and the arrest
23	☐	Luke 23	Jesus is crucified
24	☐	Luke 24	The resurrection and ascension of Jesus

Reading through St John's Gospel

Day	Tick Box	Chapter	
1	☐	John 1	John the Baptist and Jesus
2	☐	John 2	The wedding at Cana
3	☐	John 3	Nicodemus visits Jesus
4	☐	John 4	Jesus and the woman from Samaria
5	☐	John 5	The Jews reject Jesus
6	☐	John 6	Jesus is the bread of life
7	☐	John 7	Jesus is the living water
8	☐	John 8	Jesus is the light of the world
9	☐	John 9	Jesus heals a blind man
10	☐	John 10	Jesus is the good shepherd
11	☐	John 11	Jesus brings Lazarus back to life
12	☐	John 12	Jesus enters Jerusalem
13	☐	John 13	Jesus washes his disciples' feet
14	☐	John 14	Jesus answers Thomas, Philip and Judas
15	☐	John 15	Jesus is the true vine
16	☐	John 16	Jesus promises the Holy Spirit
17	☐	John 17	Jesus prays to his Father
18	☐	John 18	Jesus is put on trial
19	☐	John 19	Jesus is crucified
20	☐	John 20	The risen Jesus is seen
21	☐	John 21	Jesus speaks to Peter